The Wisdom of My Grandmothers

The Wisdom of My Grandmothers

Adriana Trigiani

W F HOWES LTD

This large print edition published in 2012 by
W F Howes Ltd
Unit 4, Rearsby Business Park, Gaddesby Lane,
Rearsby, Leicester LE7 4YH

1 3 5 7 9 10 8 6 4 2

First published in the United Kingdom in 2012
by Simon & Schuster UK Ltd

A CIP catalogue record for this book is available
from the British Library

ISBN 978 1 47120 187 5

Typeset by Palimpsest Book Production Limited,
Falkirk, Stirlingshire
Printed and bound in Great Britain
by MPG Books Ltd, Bodmin, Cornwall

MIX
Paper from
responsible sources
FSC
www.fsc.org   FSC® C018575

For Lucia

Adriana Trigiani
New York City
May 5, 2010

CONTENTS

CONTENTS

INTRODUCTION

INTRODUCTION

Luck is a wily thing. You can have a run of it, or get hit once and hard with the lucky stick, or luck may always seem like that handsome stranger across a crowded room, completely out of reach, even when you're wearing your best party dress and lipstick. You can see luck when others have it, but you know it's not your turn. Sometimes it appears that luck is a birthright, making someone else's life seemed charmed from the outset. Luck is usually seen from a distance, from a place of want.

Not so for me.

I was truly lucky to have been given two stellar grandmothers, Lucia Spada Bonicelli (Lucy) and Yolanda Perin Trigiani (Viola). They showed me, in their own ways, how to get out of my own way and carve out a fulfilling life,

> a peaceful life,
> a gracious life,
> and
> a secure life.

My grandmothers bestowed on me, through their examples, the importance of developing *character*, rooted in kindness; and a *spirit* that might negotiate loss and rebound from grief to love more deeply. Their hope was that my spirit would serve to reinforce character when I fell short, made mistakes, or hurt someone I cared about through my own actions. For them, faith was the result of working through the spirit, and a tool, a means to go inward.

In dark moments when despair kicks joy to the curb, and I feel I don't have it in me to go one more step, I turn to my grandmothers for strength. In my memory are moments, glistening pop beads, the kind I played with as a girl. I string them together now in my mind's eye and hold them close. They are not jewels to keep in a vault nor ones that would withstand any sort of appraisal. These are functional pearls, iridescent and simple in their beauty, yet indestructible. Unbreakable.

As I remember my grandmothers, I marvel at how they spent their time, and how they chose to fill up the years of their long lives. As women, our time is often ruled by the needs of those around us, but when I picture them, it's never in a crowd, but alone in a window or a doorway. They survived loss and times of deep sorrow, but they would tell you that they were lucky too. They earned their luck by the labor of their own hands and their determination to see a goal through to completion.

Lucia and Viola poured themselves into the

things they made, whether it was strands of fresh spaghetti or a wedding gown of duchess satin. They tended their gardens and their children. They built their companies and their relationships. They made time, they made things, they made a *life.*

The life lessons my grandmothers taught me help me stay the course, and here on these pages, I hope their wisdom might inspire you too. The past has a patina. Once the colors were bright and now they have faded. But looking closely now, from a distance, the details emerge richer in tone and texture, and ever more lovely in memory.

Adriana Trigiani
New York City
2010

CHAPTER 1

VIOLA

Yolanda Perin Trigiani (Viola) stood at five feet five inches, but seemed much taller because she was short-waisted and had long legs. In her youth, she wore wide-brimmed hats, festooned with peacock plumes and adornments (silk flowers, bands of grosgrain, velvet berries), making her appear taller still. Even as a girl she had mature, striking looks and a serious countenance. Her ancestry was apparent in her strong profile, upright posture, and quick stride. 'Here comes the Venetian,' they'd say when she walked down Garibaldi Avenue in Roseto, Pennsylvania.

Viola's thick, jet-black hair fell in smooth waves. She had a square jaw, a prominent nose with a high bridge, dark brown eyes that were neither large nor limpid, but dark and intense, with a downcast lid (later in life, she contemplated an eye job when her lids became heavy, and it was difficult to read or to see stitch work up close, but decided against the surgery). She had beautiful lips, straight, strong white teeth, and a wide smile.

Think Joan Crawford.

My grandfather, Michael (nicknamed 'Dick'),

thought his Viola was an Italian version of the stunning star.

In fact, there was a bit of Hollywood stardust to their early courtship – their first date was to the movies to see Joan Crawford in *Montana Moon*. (By the way, Viola argued years later that they saw *Carolina Moon*. When I checked the chronology and told her that Joan Crawford made a movie in 1931 called *Montana Moon*, my grandmother replied, 'I was there. It was *Carolina Moon*.' Oh, well.)

My grandparents met when they were in their early twenties (he was four years older than she) in a pants factory in Bangor, Pennsylvania. She was tagged as a leader early on. She excelled as a machine operator, then was promoted to forelady by the age of sixteen. By the time she met my grandfather, she was a pro, with a few years of management experience under her belt and fifty operators to oversee. She mastered every machine on the floor, knew how to get the best out of her operators, and managed them to exceed their numbers and output. Operators that worked under her remember her clear, distinctive voice, which could be heard over the loud buzz of machines in the factory.

Viola and Michael's love story was fraught with near misses. My grandfather left for a time and worked in mills as a machinist first in the Bronx and then in Connecticut. Viola thought she'd lost him for good. But he eventually returned to his

2

hometown, the factory, and to her, and, in 1932, they married.

Michael Anthony Trigiani had southern Italian (Bari) good looks, dark hair, full lips, and gray eyes. In pictures, he also seems matinee-idol handsome to me, but that may be Viola's influence on the subject.

Back when she was wooing my grandfather, Viola would make him lunch every day and leave it for him in the pressing room. Those lunches became a theme with her. She made Italian delicacies, small, elegant sandwiches made with roasted peppers or thin-sliced capicola on the best bread, buttered lightly and wrapped in bleached, pressed cotton. There were ginger cookies, the size of a quarter, or slices of almond-scented pound cake, or oil pretzels, and always fresh fruit, figs, oranges, or a banana. There were thermoses of hot coffee, or bottles of cold soda. She thought of everything – utensils, napkins, portable ambience.

At the end of the workday, Viola would pick up the empty basket and take it home to repeat the process the next morning. I wondered what my grandfather's coworkers thought when their tough forelady extended this loving and gentle gesture to the man she loved each day.

Viola packed lunches throughout her life for all occasions: hampers loaded for long car trips, goody baskets left on doorsteps for someone in need, and later on, meals on-the-go for social excursions, including her gambling runs with her senior girlfriends to Atlantic City. Viola was not a warm, fuzzy character, but she showed her generosity and caring in those picnic hampers.

Viola was proud of her homemaking skills, even though she was never exclusively a homemaker. She was a working girl who became a working woman, ultimately co-owning her own blouse factory with my grandfather. A deeper meaning of the partnership was apparent in the name of the company: the Yolanda Manufacturing Company. Her ambition and determination was the engine, the driving force behind the founding of the mill, and the energy field that would sustain it for twenty-six years.

Viola had the guts and the vision to make the leap from dutiful employee to boss. She also had the work ethic and, now, the experience to court business and satisfy the buyer with a great product. My grandparents were good partners for one another; he was strong, intelligent, and possessed an easygoing nature, while she was a relentless fighter and a demanding boss. My grandfather attracted the investors to put them in business, but Viola's fine reputation guaranteed that the mill would turn out excellent-quality blouses, on time and without error.

Years later, when she'd recount the history of the founding of her factory, she always gave credit to the three men who lent them the seed money to open the factory. She didn't rest until she'd paid them back, with interest. While she worked off

4

the debt, she managed to run the mill, and also build a family. There was never any question in her mind that she would work after marriage, and would have help with child care for her four children.

For Viola the very nature of femininity was tied to the skills acquired to create a gracious home life. Family meant nurturing, and sustenance meant good food, so she became an expert baker and an excellent cook. Like most farmer's daughters of her day, they ate from their garden, and survived the winters by creating meals around fruits and vegetables they had canned.

Viola canned jams and jellies, Italian peppers with *alige* (anchovies), and sweet pickles. She also 'put up' tomatoes, enough that each child (and by extension, their children) in her immediate family would receive cases of peeled and crushed tomatoes every summer after the harvest. Viola sent enough mason jars of tomatoes to make gravy for an entire year, enough to last until the following summer, when the process was repeated.

Viola, a math whiz, was so good with figures, she could add up what she was spending in the grocery as she shopped. She would maintain a running tally in her head until she made it to the checkout counter. I was amazed when the total on the cash register was within a dollar of her prediction. So it went with the cases of tomatoes – all of her children received exactly what they needed, calculated by how many children each had. It was an uncanny knack – to know exactly what was needed, and then to provide it.

There was never any waste.

Ever.

My grandmother never threw anything away (clothing, bank records, contracts, wills, newspaper clippings, photographs; which is why I am able to write this book!). When I implored her to clean out her attic, she said, 'What if I need that ribbon I saved someday?' She even saved the sheets of wax paper from cereal boxes. When unfolded and pressed, they were the perfect size on which to cool and stack the handmade crepes she made for manicotti shells.

Viola honored her tools and took care of them. In the deep drawers of her kitchen were her mother's utensils – she used the same wooden-handled eggbeater and rolling pin that her mother had used back on the farm in Delabole. Viola took such excellent care of them, I use them today.

Viola's home was clean, neat, and orderly. She had a touch of an old-fashioned Mother Superior in her, as well as a hint of a grunt novitiate. She knew how to scrub, swab, and rinse like a nun working off a Lenten penance. There was something downright military about her approach to cleaning. When she taught me how to scrub a floor, she would wring out the moppeen with such force, the rag would be dry when she handed it to me. Her upper-body strength stayed with her to her death in the spring of her ninetieth year.

There was a duality in her approach to life, as she ran the factory and her home on parallel rails. She was a powerhouse in the mill, a taskmaster of a boss, unyielding in her quest for perfection. She worked through sick days and holiday weekends, and made no apologies for wanting to make 'good money.' If an operator was absent, Viola would sit down at the machine and cover for her. There was no difference in her mind between the manager and the employee. Her belief was that you got the job done – no matter what. But as driven as she was at work, she was just as insistent about being feminine: charming, interesting, socially engaging, and – the highest dream of all – elegant. American glamour was a goal. She believed sophistication was achieved by being an excellent hostess.

Viola lived in four homes in her lifetime. Her parents emigrated from the Veneto on their wedding day in 1906, after a short stint with relatives, and moved into a two-room house with a slate roof in Delabole, where Viola was born a year later. The rent on their home was $3.00 a month, which the newlyweds could manage because Viola's father went to work in the Slate Quarry immediately. Eventually, they moved close by to a farm set amid the rolling hills of northeastern Pennsylvania where the family grew to include five more children.

Viola's father, Davide, was a hardy but tender soul, loaded with ambition. Viola told me he worked from morning until night without complaint, pulling double duty on the farm and in the slate quarry. Viola's determination came from his example, and was also born of necessity. When Viola's mother died young at forty-three from pneumonia, the responsibility of running the home fell to her, as well as the care of the baby of the family, only five years old.

Delabole farm was rustic yet lovely. There was a barn with cows (my great-grandfather made a good living supplementing his income from the local slate quarries by delivering milk during the Great Depression through his company, Slate Springs Farm). There was a hay silo, an old red barn for the horses, and a springhouse. The yard around the house was lumpy with rocks, but the goats kept the grass at a manageable length.

There were no touches of opulence, no chandelier over the kitchen table, no fancy lamps or silk curtains. The farmhouse was comfortable and clean, with linoleum floors that could take a daily mop-down. Viola wrote, 'We children attended the school across the road where our teacher taught eight grades. I went to school at the age of four not knowing a word of English. The teacher asked my name. I said, 'Yola,' so she named me "Viola."'

When Viola married, she moved to town, four miles away, into a charming brick home at 37 Dewey Street in Roseto, Pennsylvania, with a back-yard where she planted a garden and could hang out the wash. They bought the de rigueur 1930s furniture suite in dark Victorian mahogany, like other young couples in Roseto. She replaced the linoleum floors of her youth with polished wood covered by wool rugs.

In 1952, when her children were still young, Viola moved with her family to Flicksville, a small village outside Roseto, and into the home of their dreams, a Tudor built by a Bethlehem Steel executive, set high on a hill with an in-ground swimming pool on a few acres surrounded by lush woods. My grandfather, having grown up on Garibaldi Avenue in Roseto, was ready for a change, far enough away but not too far from his roots. As it turned out, neither Viola nor her husband Michael ventured far from their birthplaces. Only a few miles separate Roseto, Delabole, and Flicksville. My grandparents were buried in Roseto, a short walk from their first home as a married couple on Dewey Street.

Flicksville was their final home. They enjoyed the setting, and poured a lot of effort into the upkeep of the land. Viola loved the house too, and lucky for her, it was closer to their mill in Martins Creek.

I remember her kitchen.

Ornate thick wooden doors, the kind you'd expect to find in an English castle, led into Viola's kitchen from a slate-covered stoop in the back of the house, next to the garage and off the driveway. The color scheme was pure 1950s: aqua and Pepto-Bismol pink. There was pink straw wallpaper, and brown walnut cabinetry with black hinges shaped like swords held by armored knights.

9

The linoleum floor was starstruck, literally – wide stripes of aqua and pink inset with shiny brass stars.

The kitchen was small by today's standards, but it contained absolutely everything Viola needed to turn out dinner parties for twenty guests or more. (Full disclosure: in the basement below the kitchen was a 'canning kitchen' with a stove in the laundry room typical of many Italian American homes.) In the official upstairs kitchen were two generous countertops with recessed lighting for prep and assembly. There was a deep stainless steel double sink framed by windows, a four-burner electric stove, and an oven set into the wall, surrounded by more cabinetry. Tucked into a corner was a small pink linoleum desk in an alcove with a pink phone hanging on the wall, the phone number printed on the circular dial: 588-5746. It had an extra-long spiral of pink cord so Viola could talk on the phone and cook at the same time.

In the connecting breakfast nook sat a table built by my grandfather and two straight walnut benches, by a big window that overlooked the grounds. On the opposite wall stood a plate armoire, made by a carpenter friend of my grandfather's. A series of plates depicting foxhunting scenes in the English countryside were centered carefully in the dish grooves.

My Italian grandparents aspired to the British style, from the chintz teacups to the chocolate brown crossbeams set in beige stucco on the facade of the Tudor. For them, all things British meant aristocratic. Whenever Viola admired a well-turned-out gentleman, she said, 'He was like a duke.' And when a woman did the same, 'She was a queen.' The royal touch went one step further. Underneath the floor, at the foot of the dining room table (Viola's seat), was a servant bell that, when pressed, dinged in the kitchen to summon the help. Usually, 'the help' was a blood relative of the hostess.

From this small kitchen, Viola produced gorgeous dinner parties. She served canapés and cocktails in the living room (aqua and gray decor) first. Viola made a mean Manhattan, and as kids, we'd fish out the maraschino cherries after the grown-ups went into the dining room to eat. The canapés were pure charcuterie, slender slices of Italian salami, juicy olives, fresh local scamorza (a locally made version of mozzarella, braided by hand) dusted with black pepper, served with small biscuits and fresh bread.

The first course was always one of her hearty soups (Italian wedding soup with greens) followed by a salad, made with fresh greens tossed with a simple oil and vinegar dressing I cannot duplicate (I only know she never used black pepper, only salt, to season a salad). She went through phases where she'd come upon a new recipe and perfect the dish by repeating it over the course of a year's worth of dinner parties. She went on a jag in the 1970s where she made oysters Rockefeller in actual seashells. This was a perfect dish to serve with a Fuzzy Navel, a fresh aperitif made with peach schnapps.

The main course usually harkened back to meals prepared during her youth on the farm: creamy polenta with a robust tomato sauce tinged with cinnamon, savory meatballs and sausage with her handmade manicotti (filling and crêpes), or a Venetian fish brodetto in a marinara sauce that I crave to this day.

For dessert, she made fruit pies from scratch, simple pound cakes and cookies from her sister-in-law Gus's oeuvre (Italian sesame cookies, small chocolate cups, and ginger cookies we called 'dunkers'). There was no fancy frosting or rosettes of whipped cream – she was as direct in her baking techniques as she was on the factory floor. She used the freshest and best ingredients, never a box mix or prefab dough. Her devotion to eating fresh was a lifelong commitment; we used to drive to a nearby farm early in the morning so she might have the freshest eggs for baking. The Miller Egg Ranch operated on the honor system; you took what you needed and left the exact change in a cup.

Viola was a regular at Calandra's in Nazareth, Pennsylvania, where they made fresh ricotta, mozzarella, and grated Romano cheese. When my dad decided to move his young family from Pennsylvania to Big Stone Gap, Virginia, she said, 'I could never live in a place where they don't make cheese.'

After dessert, she served digestifs (bitters, Fernet Branca, Amaretto, or Fra Angelico) from a standard 1950s rolling liquor cart with two shelves. There was always a large carved wooden bowl filled with nuts and studded with silver nutcrackers and matching picks to remove the meat from the nuts, placed on the table after dessert. Viola even had a fancy table-size silver-handled whisk broom and dustpan to sweep up the shells.

After dinner and dishes, there was usually a card game, and sometimes there was just conversation, but I remember feeling content after one of her dinner parties, hoping the night would never end. We laughed a lot. Viola played records on the hi-fi before and after dinner, stacking the LPs of Frank Sinatra, Dean Martin, One Thousand and One Strings, and other instrumentals. The hi-fi still works because none of her sixteen grandchildren was ever allowed to play it.

I once asked her how she knew how to throw dinner parties. After all, her own mother had died so young, and all Viola knew was life on the farm. She did not have exposure to fancy restaurants or grand parties, yet she knew how to prepare elegant dishes and entertain with style. Viola admitted she studied how people entertained in the movies ('the show') and learned how to create a dinner party from a small series of books she received when she married.

The Woman's Library was created by Social Culture Publications in New York City in the

1920s as a series of advice books for young ladies who aspired to be proper hostesses, entertain like the upper classes, and present themselves with good manners. With or without these books, I doubt the queen of England herself entertained her guests better than my grandmother. And I'll bet the cooks at Buckingham Palace couldn't top her polenta.

Everything I Ever Wanted

Long summer days were workdays for Viola, as they were loaded with light, perfect for hanging laundry on the clothes-line, baking, and cleaning. Viola rose early, and often started her day berry picking.

One summer morning, before daybreak, Viola drove her station wagon, the back loaded with empty baskets, on a winding road through Flicksville with walls of green corn on either side. She was on her way to a commercial farm loaded with strawberry fields, where you could pick your own and pay for them. Her baby sister, Lavinia, had the same idea. She too rose early, drove to the farm, grabbed a stack of empty baskets from her car trunk, and waited for the flatbed truck to take her up the hill to the fields filled with the ripest berries.

As the sun came up over the mountain, Lavinia saw the truck coming down the dirt road toward her. As it appeared in the distance, she saw a lone rider with her legs dangling over the side of the flatbed, surrounded by baskets filled with fresh picked strawberries. It was my grandmother, well into her seventies, wearing cutoff jean shorts, a vibrant polyester blouse, and a sun hat. When she saw her baby sister, she said, 'You're late.'

Viola's routine was to return to her kitchen with the fresh-picked berries and commence making pies, crust first. Viola's fruit pies were works of art, sweet fruit in a delicate, lacy crust. I never remember a slice left over, they were eaten the day they were baked. She loathed sleeping late, didn't understand it, never did it, and thought it a terrible waste of time. 'I don't understand why anybody would waste the morning,' she'd say. To this day, as a result of her example (and insistence), I can't sleep late. I still get a vision of my grandmother's face, much like Saint Thomas Aquinas had when he saw the face of God promising eternal life in exchange for a purposeful life. Once I've seen The Face, I have to get up. And, like Viola, I need eight to ten hours of sleep, so early to bed is a house rule. 'It's time for the Lily White party,' Viola used to say around eight in the evening. Some party. Sleep was part of her master plan to get more work out of you the following day. This good habit sustains me, and now I've passed the habit along to my daughter.

A particular summer day at Viola's house stands out in my memory. I am one of seven children, Viola is one of six herself, so we shared the big-family dynamic. Therefore it was rare that we were alone, just the two of us. But on this particular day, we were. I was in college and was spending the summer with her, and had a job as a fry cook in a local restaurant. I had one day off a week, and Viola looked at my day of rest as an opportunity to get things done around the house.

So I washed her car.

Cars in particular, their care and maintenance, were important to Viola; they were an outward sign of opulence and another gleaming ray of the sun called the American dream. She told me about my grandfather's car on their first date, and how much she admired it (running boards, rumble seat). Various photographs of her from the age of sixteen feature her in the foreground, and a car gleaming in the background, the ultimate sign of working class success.

Throughout her life, she took care of her cars like jewels. Cars were markers of particular eras in Viola's life, and memories were built around them. In the late 1920s, Viola drove a Nash Roadster. My grandparents owned a Packard in the 1940s, the 'it' car of the moment, and then moved on to Cadillacs, the ultimate stature vehicle, American designed and built, like the blouses in the factory. When I was little, their 1962 Cadillac Sedan de Ville was charcoal gray with fins, with a pale silver leather interior. Her 1960s work car, a Ford station wagon painted dull gold, was often filled with bundles of blouses that needed sleeves turned, or tickets affixed. When her grandsons bought her a car later in life, it was returned to them in pristine condition upon her death, plastic seat covers intact. When my father graduated from college, the first in his family to do so, they gave him a mint-green 1954 Pontiac convertible. A car was the highest reward you could get in the Trigiani family.

But that summer I was washing Viola's 1970s car, a Mercury Grand Marquis four-door sedan, paying special attention to the hubcaps with a scrub brush. You would think that washing a car is not something you have to learn how to do, but Viola had taught me her technique years earlier and her expectation was that I would follow orders. She didn't leave my efforts to chance. She oversaw my progress through the kitchen window. Once a forelady, forever a forelady. She did not restrain herself when it came to pointing out any missed spots.

Viola maintained her car's interior no differently from her own living room. We dusted, swept, vaccumed, and buffed. The carpet mats were shampooed. Then, once the interior passed her inspection, and before you scrubbed the outside of the car, Viola would take a squeezed lemon from the kitchen and set it on the dashboard, close the doors, and let the summer sun fill the car with a fresh lemon scent. (Throw the lemon out when it turns black. On a hot summer day, that takes about fifteen minutes.)

To wash the exterior of a car, begin with two

buckets of water, one spritzed with dish detergent (not too much, just a quick blast of soap), the other bucket with clean water. Have a garden hose close by. You also need a scrub brush for the hub caps, a bottle of bleach to whiten the rims, a cup of white vinegar to add to the clean, cold bucket of water for polishing the bumpers (later), and a pile of moppeens (old dish towels).

Begin by swabbing the roof (without missing any spots!), then the hood, then the sides, and finally the windows. Soak the moppeens in the soapy bucket, with big circular motions cover an area, and then in straight rows, with rags dipped in the rinse bucket, cover the same areas. Hose off the car, making sure you leave no soapy residue behind. Commence the detail work: bleach the rims (scrub brush and Clorox) and polish the chrome (vinegar, cold water, and more fresh moppeens).

By the time I was finished, Viola's lime green land yacht glistened like a pale emerald.

I was beat. But she wasn't. Even at the end of a long day, I never saw her energy flag. She baked pies while I polished the bumpers, and with the hot sun over the hill, she jumped on the riding lawn mower and mowed the trim of her property. I can see her, weaving in and out of the property line like a whipstitch, the soft whirl of the motor in the distance. She was meticulous about her yard, and you'd often seeing her striding across the acreage collecting sticks. (If I was ever bored as a kid, she'd say, 'Go pick up sticks.' Evidently,

you don't want sticks getting in the mower blades.)
Viola took such pride in her green rolling hills;
her lawn was treated more delicately than an
antique Aubusson. She had a war going with the
indigenous groundhogs, and took it personally
when they'd bore holes in her yard or eat from
her garden.

Viola was a good shot, and owned several rifles,
which she did not hesitate to use when a groundhog
had the temerity to lumber into the open. I can
see her, rifle cocked into the crook of her shoulder,
her steely eyes squinting behind her eyeglasses,
pale blue octagon frames so large they resembled
windshield wipers (Dame Edna owns the other
pair) as she tracked the vermin through the view-
finder on the gun. She was convinced that the
groundhog came above ground to taunt her, so
retaliation was necessary. When she'd pull the
trigger, she'd hold the flank of the gun steady, so
there was no recoil as there can be in police dramas
on television. She was in total control, of the gun
and the groundhog. The guns always made me
nervous, and I declined to learn how to use one,
even though she offered to teach me. Washing cars
seemed safer.

By late afternoon the laundry, hung on the line
in the morning, was ready to come down. Folding
her bleached sheets was like folding cardboard.
She never used fabric softener ('It gums up the
machine,' she'd say). She was an early environ-
mentalist. Viola was green before anyone thought

about being green. Every day was Earth Day for Viola. She loved a low electricity bill and a wee water bill. It was a badge of honor for her to employ Mother Nature instead of Mother Maytag.

'Don't you feel good?' she said to me on that summer day, inhaling the fresh Pennsylvania air. I didn't want to admit I was exhausted, because she didn't believe in it, so I lied and said, 'Like a million bucks.'

'Come on,' she said.

I followed her into the kitchen. She took two crystal tumblers out of the cupboard and went for the liquor cart. She took the gold shaker and commenced making a killer batch of her Manhattans. Like a scientist making a brew to save mankind, she'd measure (by eye) sweet vermouth, whiskey, and a few tablespoons of cherry juice into the shaker. Then she'd gently shake the concoction like she was rattling maracas in a Carmen Miranda kick line.

She put the shaker aside ('Let it rest,' she said), and made our hors d'oeuvres: thin slices of fresh mozzarella, the ends of some crusty Italian bread drizzled with a bit of olive oil. Then she took out a canister and put a couple of oil pretzels she had made on the tray. (These resemble popovers with a hard-shell crust. When you bite into them, they are spongy and not too sweet – perfect with a cocktail.)

She poured the Manhattans into the ice-filled tumblers, added two cherries to each glass, and said, 'Let's go.' She carried the drinks outside, and I followed with the snacks.

She usually took cocktail hour on her folding chair under the shade tree by the kitchen window. But on this day, I felt compelled to break her routine.

'Let's go sit in the field,' I said, grabbing a garden chair with my free hand, and we walked toward the top of the hill overlooking Viola's lawn. The fringe of towering pine trees around the property seemed as tall as a city skyline. The low wall of fieldstone in the distance looked lavender as the late afternoon summer sky turned the color of a ripe peach. I lay down on the grass while Viola sat in the lawn chair.

Viola had lived alone since my grandfather died. If she was ever lonesome, she never let on. Somehow, caring for the home she'd lived in with her husband and continuing his efforts to keep the land in perfect shape gave her a deep sense of fulfillment. Her home meant everything to her. She prayed to never have to leave it. Viola never got over the fact that she lived in this majestic Tudor, that she owned it outright, so she took care of it like a castle, a steward of the house and the land, knowing her time in it was precious and now fleeting.

We sipped our cocktails and talked. Our relationship had changed over the years. At first I was in awe of her, then scared of her, but eventually she became my friend. These were the years I would love the best, when I was young and she still seemed to be. She had short, wavy, silver hair now, and her knees were bowed from arthritis, but in every other respect, it appeared she had not changed in the twenty years since I was born. She was still gutsy, and in fact she got more so as time went on. It was as if she wasn't going to let anything get her, not old age nor sickness nor death. For a long time, I imagined that she'd never die. If anyone could skirt death, it would be Viola, by sheer determination.

When she saw an elderly lady (around her age) crossing the street slowly, she turned to me and said, 'She's not slow because of her age. That one moved like a turtle when she was young.' Viola would not accept old age as an excuse for giving up or giving in. She had her armor on.

The sun began to slip over the Blue Mountains. Hot summer days in northeastern Pennsylvania cool off quickly at twilight, and the temperature was near perfect. The sky colors were like an Impressionist masterpiece, saturated blues with streaks of lilac, soft corals hemmed in milky beige. I could see the first flickers of fireflies in the trees. Even the cocktail turned more beautiful in this light. The cherries glowed at the bottom of the amber mixture.

This was bliss.

I'm not much of a drinker, but Viola's cocktails were delicious; they had a woodsy taste that burned my lips (the whiskey, evidently), but then went down sweet (the vermouth) and cold, as a lovely and immediate buzz ensued. After the chores that culminated in washing the car, I came to appreciate that lovely buzz. It meant we were finally off the clock; miracle of miracles, there was nothing left to do around the house.

'Every once in a while, have a drink,' she said. 'When you've earned it.'

This advice comes from the same grandmother who sent me a tin of her cookies when I was in college. The note said, 'Eat one cookie at a time.' I'm still not quite sure how to eat them otherwise. (Viola's letter provided great entertainment to my roommate Cynthia, for whom I gave readings of the letters in our dorm room at Saint Mary's. Cynthia, raised by steel magnolias from Alabama, said, 'Dang. Your grandmothuh has mine beat. Mah grandmothuh sends me a tin of cheese straws, but she nevuh tells me how to eat 'em.')

There is nothing like the quiet in the country; you can think, and you can breathe. The scent of sweet grass hangs in the air and every once in a while the night-blooming jasmine plays through like delicate perfume on a sophisticated woman. I didn't crave nature or peace and quiet in my youth, but now I understand my grandmother's need for it. It gets harder and harder to *think* amid the noise of the world, and lately it seems that the volume dial has been cranked to the max. I look back on my time with Viola and remember the value of silence.

Viola was lucky enough to find a place she could make sacred. She'd had this kind of peace on the farm as a girl, and now, in her advancing years, she retrieved it, held on to it like the best of her memories. Her home became her final passion and mission; she was determined to hold on to that house, the rolling hillsides, and the fringe of forest. As luck would have it, she never had to leave the place she loved – she lived there until she died.

'Did you ever think you might remarry?' I asked her.

'Never,' she said.

'You never had a date after Grandpop died?'

'No. Although I did let a man buy me a hot dog in Atlantic City once.'

'That's not a date, Gram.'

'I guess not.' She sipped her drink. 'You know, when I brought Grandpop home from Rochester...'

In a last-ditch effort to save my grandfather's life, my grandmother took him to the Mayo Clinic in the spring of 1968. They had heard of experimental cancer treatments, and Grandpop's local doctor recommended he try them. They went to Minnesota and tried the new treatments, drastic radiation sessions and chemotherapy, but it soon became clear that were not going to work. So, at Viola's insistence, the doctors stopped the treatments. They flew home, so my grandfather could die in peace with his family around him.

'We flew home from Minnesota,' she said. 'And we were sitting on the plane. And your grandfather said, "You're young, Viola."' She was sixty years old at the time. 'And you've got a couple of bucks. Be careful.'

And then she said to him, 'Don't worry about me. I had everything I ever wanted.'

This was one of their last conversations. As soon as my grandfather returned home to his bed, he stopped speaking entirely. Viola's diary tells me that he died at 8:15 that evening. (This entry was the last she ever wrote, even though she lived twenty-nine years beyond his death.)

I knew, around this time of day, when the work was done and the cocktails were poured, she missed my grandfather. I also knew that as the years passed, she missed him *more*, not less. She had regrets, but she was a widow who wasn't going to make things right by finding a new husband and growing through new experiences. Her job was to keep everything nice – the garden, the house, the property – and all of that effort was in his honor. She had a sense that it was her duty to continue to make him proud, even though he was not here to enjoy her efforts.

Viola was not a sentimental woman, though she could be moved to tears by Lifetime movies and photographs of missing children on milk cartons. Love wasn't something she talked about, but rather would *show*, by making a meal that would please my grandfather, shipping a perfect lot of blouses from the mill, or meeting payroll. I don't believe they talked about their feelings very much, from the things Viola told me, but it was clear they acted upon them. They *showed* their love for one another. Even though their temperaments were different and they had individual approaches to problem solving, they had an underlying devotion to one another and their marriage. Viola saved the cards and telegrams he sent to her, and more telling (at least to me), Michael saved those she had sent to him. Reading them now, I understand how they felt about one another. They did not have an easy time of it. Viola's ambition was an ongoing challenge for him, and I'm sure he sometimes hoped for a more traditional wife. At least, this is what Viola told me.

Viola, despite her proud demeanor, had a *heart*, and in her own way she could articulate the details of the rooms in it in a way that an artist might, in one brushstroke in a single perfect shade. She had regrets, she'd later share, but she knew what they were and why she had them. She told me she had made many mistakes, with her husband, her children, her grandchildren, and her employees. Those regrets often kept her up at night, and when I would visit, she'd wake me up to talk them through. She believed in atonement, but mourned that she could not atone once those she loved had died. Viola never practiced self-deception; she was as clear in her thinking as the cloudless sky. Viola owned up to her shortcomings – or at least, she did to me.

I was lying on the grass, next to her in the chair, a summer snow angel at this point, stretched out and one with the earth beneath me, as though I was carved into it. My arms were behind my head, pretzeled to make a pillow. The crystal tumbler rested in the grass like a jewel.

Suddenly there was a great whooshing sound. I sat up and surveyed the sky. There was another blast of this strange sound I'd never heard before, but no movement. We looked in the direction of the forest, a expanse of green trees beyond the property line, but the leaves on the trees were still.

The noise grew louder.

I looked up at Viola; she was more curious than scared. She wasn't always so trusting of the universe. When I was a girl, she made us stay indoors one summer when it was reported that bits of Skylab had broken off from the lunar station. NASA determined that errant shards of metal might drop into the earth's atmosphere, through the clouds, and onto children playing outside in northeastern Pennsylvania. That was the summer I learned how to embroider.

But this day she didn't run into the house, nor did she advise me to seek cover. She sat there calmly and looked to the origin of the sound. I followed her gaze up and over the trees.

Suddenly, in the purple sky, the edge of something massive, round, and strawberry red rose from the green forest. It grew larger and larger, towering over the height and breadth of the tree line below it.

This mighty red thing cleared the treetops and revealed itself. It was a hot air balloon, with a dangling gold basket suspended on cords, climbing higher and higher into the sky. As it sailed over us and then out of sight, I looked up at her.

'Are we drunk?' I asked her.

And she said, 'No. Just lucky.'

CHAPTER 2

LUCIA

Lucia Spada was born in Schilpario, Italy, on Christmas Day, 1894. The Spada family lived high in the Italian Alps, above the city of Bergamo, which is north of Milan in the Lombardy region. Lucia stood five-seven and was trim, with strong legs. She had refined northern Italian features – an oval face with large, dark brown eyes, accented by thick, well-shaped eyebrows, a razor-straight nose, full lips, and high cheekbones.

Lucia was the eldest of eight children. Her childhood was marked by tragedy, when her beloved five-year-old sister Margarita (Rita) died suddenly of an illness. The family that remained struggled to survive, as did all families at the turn of the twentieth century in the mountains of Italy. Her father, Marco, looked for work to supplement the income he made from running a horse-and-buggy service from Schilpario to Bergamo. Marco was stern, a perfectionist with a creative streak that made him a bit of an inventor with a hunger for world travel. His wife, Giacomina, was a sweet and tender mother who made a comfortable home life despite their poverty.

The notion of Marco running a buggy service in the Alps was enchanting until I went up the mountain to Schilapario myself, decades later. A single narrow, winding road cuts through the mountain, with hefty ceilings of stone overhead, only to sweep out from the underpass and create a harrowing path on the edge of the mountain itself. The road weaves in and out in this fashion all the way to the top, past Val de Scalve and up to Schilpario, where villages are carved out in the hills as if in relief.

High in the Alps, the vistas are majestic. Towering trees form a swirling skyline against a swath of deep blue. At night the full moon looks like a sugar cookie, and seems so close, you might reach up and break off a piece of it. By day, the colors of the landscape are painterly in the light, a waxy green palette of wide, deep fields with clusters of bright yellow and dark purple from local flowers like edelweiss. At sundown, the Alpine sky turns a deep inky blue, and the stars over northern Italy shimmer like flecks of gold.

As heavenly as it is to look from the curves up to the peaks, it's utterly terrifying to look down. The gorges between the steep mountain walls are so deep, it is impossible to see the bottom. Great shards of rock stick out from the valley walls like teeth.

I imagined a horse and buggy on that mountain, in the snow and rain, and wondered how Marco survived. From the distance of decades, I could appreciate his notoriously stern demeanor. Lucia's father worked in a state of constant anxiety, and his wife's was probably worse.

Circumstances became so terrible for the Spada family that by 1917, Lucia volunteered to go to the United States with her father to find work. The plan was to send the money they made home to Schilpario, and then, when they had saved enough, Marco and Lucia would return and buy a house so that the family would be, at long last, secure. The plan was made quickly as they always are when a situation is dire. The Spadas had a cousin in Hoboken, New Jersey, who would put them up and help them find work. This begins the story of Lucia, who, once in United States, insisted upon being called Lucy, the American version of her name. She had a clear mission, and her goal was to see it through, until her family was secure.

Once Lucy and Marco arrived in New York City, after a journey where Lucia became so ill she would never board a ship again, she settled in with her cousins and got a job in a Hoboken mill as a sewing machine operator making children's clothes for $2.00 a week.

Lucy told me that she made quick work of learning English, because on the first day, the foreman came by and hollered, 'Faster, Lucy. *Faster.*' She didn't understand what he was saying, so she vowed to learn English so she could keep her job and understand what was required of her.

Soon after Lucy was settled in New Jersey, her

31

father decided to travel to find work that paid a decent wage. Marco left Hoboken for nearly two years, working around the world and saving his pay. He went to Canada, then to Argentina, on to Australia, then back to the States.

In the meantime, Lucy had fallen in love with my grandfather, Carlo Bonicelli, who was, surprisingly enough, from Vilminore, a neighboring village to Schilpario only five miles away. Though they had never met in Italy, they were bonded by their dialect, work ethic, and utter attraction for one another. There was something instantly familiar about Carlo for Lucy, they were *simpatico* and their similarities reassured her. Carlo Augustus Bonicelli was romantic and funny. His square jaw showed determination, as his soft brown eyes showed his emotional and sensitive nature.

Lucy told me years later that when she was young, a woman rarely chose her own husband; that duty was left to the family, who arranged the marriages and 'made a match.' But, she said with great pride, she and Carlo had *chosen* one another; it was a marriage based on love.

This was so important to her that she reiterated it in the last conversation I had with her.

Lucy was a serious young woman, and Carlo was the opposite. Funny, gregarious, and social, he played a mean tin bugle. Marco met his future son-in-law and, confident that his independent daughter Lucy had chosen a good man, returned to Schilpario, to his wife and family, to build the house on Via Scalina that the Spadas and their descendants still live in today.

Lucy told her new husband that she would be happy to do any job except farm. In Italy, her family kept rabbits and chickens, but part of Lucy's American dream was not to make a career of it.

Carlo was a shoemaker, and with Lucy's skills as a seamstress, they knew together they could make a living. They decided to partner with Carlo's friend, another shoemaker, Giuseppe Bonanto. The men had heard that shoemakers were in short supply on the Iron Range in Minnesota, so the two couples decided to leave New Jersey for the Midwest.

When they arrived in Buhl, Minnesota, it became clear, after a time, that there wasn't enough work for two shoemakers in town. So the men flipped a coin to decide who would move on to the next town, Chisholm, where there was a need for a shoemaker. Carlo lost the toss, and he and Lucy departed for Chisholm.

The Iron Range

Chisholm, a prim small town in northern Minnesota, on the vast Iron Range, looks from a distance like low, rolling hills of cinnamon, where the earth has been stripped to dig for iron ore. As in most American mining towns, there was work at the ready, the mines were in operation twenty-four hours a day. Day shifts blended into hoot owl (night) shifts, so the industry attracted ambitious immigrants hoping to make a living, or men like my grandfather looking to supplement their trade with an extra paycheck.

A colorful mix of Yugoslavians, Hungarians, Czechoslovakians, Italians, Polish, Russian, German, and Jewish families rounded out the community, built at first by those of Scandinavian descent. Lakes large and small surround the town, and there's a beauty right off Main Street called Long-year Lake. I remember whitecaps on that lake, when the wind blew through during summer storms. The water was deep and clear and blue.

In her lifetime, Lucy lived for the most part in two homes: the house in which she was born, in Schilpario, and at 5 West Lake Street in Chisholm. For the last seven years of her life, she lived in Leisure Hills, a rest home in nearby Hibbing. She suffered a stroke in 1985 that left the right side of her body paralyzed, but her mind was sharp until the day she died.

Carlo died when he was thirty-nine years old, and Lucy was thirty-five. She never remarried, or even went out socially with men after that. She raised her family and put all three of her children through college on the money she earned sewing and selling factory-made shoes, including the popular Red Goose brand. She believed children needed the best shoes in the family, a structured

34

leather lace-up boot to protect the growing bones and support the ankle.

Lucy wouldn't sell a pair of shoes that didn't fit properly, and always encouraged parents to buy function and fit over style. She would rather lose a sale than fit a child's foot improperly. My grandmother talked her customers out of buying shoes as much as she sold them.

At the top of the hill, the first building you see when you make the turn onto the main street of Chisholm is the public library. With the flow of income from the mines, the community built beautiful public schools, parks, and the library. My grandmother went to the library weekly, and took her children along, which is where my mom's addiction to books began; eventually she and her twin sister Irma became librarians.

I spent a lot of time in the Chisholm library one long summer in the 1970s. The architecture of the library was inviting to children; it looked like a stately red brick house. Inside, the lemon wax used to polish the walnut reading tables and the sweet scent of ink on old paper filled the spacious rooms, filled with light from the generous lead-paned windows. The building was an avid reader's dream, lots of bright, natural light, and alcoves and nooks perfect for reading uninterrupted.

In 1920 my grandparents moved into a simple red-brick building that anchored the opposite end of the wide Main Street. The establishments that my grandmother frequented on Main Street had old world charm. Hilmer's Bakery sold delicious sweets (*povitica*), doughnuts filled with jam and rolled in sugar, and dense, sweet strudels (all that Central European baking talent), the Silvestri family ran Choppy's Pizza, and a popular Italian-owned family restaurant, Valentini's, held annual dinners where they made polenta on long wooden boards.

Known for her can-do common sense and even temperament, Lucy had a place of respect in her community in matters practical and philosophical. Parents trusted her with their children. Mothers would send their children to Lucy's shop after school to wait for pickup. Her shop was a meeting point in town. People knew Lucy was typically in the shop, and her door was always open.

The places Lucy avoided, like the local bars, were plentiful. Mining and the bar life go hand in hand like mother and child. During the summers, I would pass the bars in daytime, and the scent of booze and cigarettes would waft out, reminding me that there was a busy nightlife in Chisholm, where people worked hard and relaxed after hours.

The Progressive Shoe Shop

My grandfather opened the Progressive Shoe Shop in the front room on the street level of 5 West Lake Street where he repaired shoes, built some, and dreamed of designing his own custom line. Later, Mom told me that the joke was that there was nothing progressive about the shop, but the name indicated my grandfather embraced a modern, contemporary vision for his American business. As a veteran of World War I, my grandfather was a proud soldier, and a newly minted American citizen. When he married Lucy, she became a citizen too.

Lucy's sewing shop was in the back room of the first floor. There was an open service window in the wall separating the shoe shop from her workroom. This saved Lucy a lot of time when the bells on the door would jingle and a customer would enter, and in the years before he died offered her instant communication with her husband. There was a door leading to the back room, near the checkout desk, upon which was an ornate cash register with brass bindings, bezel-set number keys, and enamel flaps with numbers that would pop up in a pane of glass when the keys were pressed.

Lucy's workroom in the back was deep and wide, with a series of windows along the back wall. The gray wooden floor bowed in the center, from age and wear. The only pops of color were from the bolts of fabrics and the pots of red geraniums along the ledges of the windows.

Her sewing machine – a black-enameled Singer painted with gold curlicues set on a sturdy wooden table – was set in the center of the room to take advantage of the light. She let me sit in her work chair and pump the foot pedal, a wrought iron plate designed with open scrollwork. Both my feet could fit, and I would pretend to drive instead of sew.

There were storage closets for her supplies, a worktable for cutting patterns, and two easy chairs for company, who would come through and chat while she worked. There was a separate washroom in the back corner.

A screen door lead to the backyard, a square patch of green with an enormous shade tree. I remember thinking that her yard was unmanicured, much like the farm in Delabole, except that of course, Lucy did not have a goat. When Carlo was alive, like her mother in Italy, she kept rabbits, but eventually she gave them up and kept a chicken coop. They ate well from the chicken coop – roast chickens (yes, my grandmother wrung their necks herself), hearty soups, and fresh eggs.

When I was a girl, Lucy rented part of the workroom to Zeke Salvini, a longtime family friend who sold linoleum. This arrangement was one of the small sidebar businesses she had through the years to supplement what she made sewing for a little extra pocket money. Along one wall of her workroom, Zeke stored big rolls of linoleum. Zeke gave me small, square samples of linoleum on a chain to play with. I think he may be partially responsible for my lust for interior decorating and subsequent swatch addiction.

Lucy lost her wedding band in the workroom in the late 1960s when she was cutting a pattern.

She was bereft, so Zeke took every one of the linoleum rolls (some twelve feet high) and unrolled them, looking for the ring. They never found it.

It's hard to believe it now, but Lucy was in her mid-seventies that summer. She did not seem her age at all, as she still worked full-time. She turned the shoe repair shop into a showroom to sell shoes after my grandfather died, keeping the sewing business going in the back. After my grandfather died, she thought about having another shoemaker come in and run the shop, but decided against it. She found additional sources of income, keeping the books for a local ice company.

Lucy told me she felt lucky that her family lived above the shop, because she could run her business and tend to her family simultaneously. She also relied on her extended family of friends: the Ongaro, Uncini, Sartori, and Latini families looked out for her children, as she did for theirs. Lucy was far from her parents and blood family, but built a community of support around herself and her children. This was a key aspect to raising a successful family alone.

Outside the showroom, a hallway led up a flight of steep, wide steps to the second floor, which was home. A window set into the wall of the kitchen (a lot like the one in the wall between the shoe shop and sewing room downstairs) overlooked the stairs, so Lucy could see who was at the entrance. These windows were time savers, and for the efficient, organized Lucy, raising a family alone and working, every moment was essential, as was security. These windows helped her screen who was coming in and out of the building.

While the building was simple in design, and surely Lucy kept it that way, one element was grand and unforgettable. Throughout her home, the ceilings were fitted with skylights in the kitchen, the bedroom, and the bath. These windows provided light, and could be propped open for fresh air, but they also served as frames for the sky, which became a moving work of art through them. The Minnesota sky would float overhead, tufts of clouds on endless blue. During storms, when the sky turned black, the lighting was magnificent to observe through the glass – after they'd been bolted shut, of course, to keep out the rain.

The living room faced Main Street. Long and rectangular, it was hemmed by a series of windows. Lucy had a long sofa and chairs in simple, durable beige wool fabric that faced a television set, and a fabulous ottoman, in circus-tent stripes, burgundy and beige leather with black piping, that I loved to play on.

Next to the living room was a hallway that connected to the front bedroom and, down the back of the building, to a kitchen on the right and another bedroom across from it.

The kitchen was all white. The skylight was centered over the table, surrounded by bright white enamel appliances. The kitchen table, a rectangle four by six feet, sat on a single engraved pedestal painted white, with matching chairs. The suite was a gift of the Morzenti family in Buhl, to express gratitude that Lucy had taken in their daughter when her mother was ill. Lucy told me that when she came to Chisholm, and through the years, that immigrant families coped by banding together, and doing for one another what family would have provided back home.

The examples of bartering among the immigrants are legendary, and it was a system where everyone benefited from the exchange. Lucy would make your curtains, and in exchange, you might build her fence. Nothing was thrown away, as there was always someone who might use what you didn't need any longer. This exchange brought a civility and network of support that my grandmother would honor all her life.

Lucy was a fine cook and baker. She made northern Italian delicacies – gnocchi, a potato-based pasta, and hand-rolled pasta – in her kitchen. There was a savory roast and vegetables with roasted potatoes, followed by a sponge cake, every Sunday after church. Lucy worked hard to provide for her family, but she didn't let on to her three children how difficult their circumstances were in the years after Carlo died. My mother remembers the Christmas after her father died, when the Salvation Army brought a basket by, with a turkey, food staples, and candy for the kids. Lucy thanked them kindly, and then instructed them to take the basket to a family who truly needed it. I can only imagine the worry she faced every night when she went to sleep, alone in a country without any family, without a husband, with three small children to raise and a business to run.

One of Lucy's solutions to saving money was to do as much labor herself as possible, including the chores around the house. While her home was warm and inviting, it wasn't fancy. She did not invest money or time in renovating, or buying the myriad of appliances that would make her life easier. When the children grew up, they did the maintenance, and my aunt Irma would paint the walls. I liked how Lucy lived, and in particular, I loved her bathroom.

The bathroom was painted a cheery yellow with a skylight positioned over the pedestal sink. There was an artful sloped roof with an alcove at the far end, a deep white enamel tub on claw feet centered in it, with a silver hose and nozzle the size of a large shower head anchored on a stainless steel holder. I never saw another tub like that one until I went to Italy. I imagine Lucy never changed the tub into a mod shower because it reminded her of home – of Schilpario.

Beyond the bathroom, there were two rooms at the back of the building – Lucy's bedroom on the far side, and opposite it, a workroom that could have easily been a fourth bedroom. Luckily Lucy had twin girls and one son, so three bedrooms was plenty. The workroom had windows along one wall. In the center of the room was a white enamel wringer washing machine, which Lucy operated herself. The deep drum of the washer would fill with water from a wide hose attached to the wall. Lucy would add detergent to the water first. The clothes would swirl around, and then, after a lengthy rinse, Lucy would put each individual item of clothing through the wringer, which looked like two metal rolling pins with a hand crank on the side.

Once the garment was put through the wringer, she'd snap it and place it on a hanger or over a rack, a series of wooden dowels along the wall. The laundry process had a Zen quality to it. Even though the work took muscle and concentration, she reveled in it. I often think of her, and how she applied the same effort to her sewing as she did to mundane tasks. All of her work, regardless of its nature, seemed to bring her a sense of satisfaction. She didn't fight against duty or chores or hard work. There wasn't any resentment around her obligations, I never heard any complaints. She moved in harmony with her chores, as if having a purpose and being useful was its own brand of art.

Because of the wringer washer, Lucy's home was always filled with the fresh scents of clean camphor, bleach, and a touch of peppermint. There was no clothes dryer, so everything that was washed was hung and then pressed. Lucy left the windows open in the workroom, as the air helped dry the clothing more quickly. In the summer, the sun would pour in and dry the clothes in double time.

On days when she wasn't doing laundry, and the pristine room was available for other uses, Lucy made pasta. She rolled her pasta by hand in the kitchen, then hung it on the clean dowels to dry.

Between her bedroom and the workroom was a door that led to a second-floor landing. That landing led to a set of wooden stairs that went two stories down to the yard. You could touch the branches of the shade tree from that landing, though I was too scared of falling to try. Lucy left that door open too, and the fresh Minnesota air would blow through her house. In fact, I remember the windows being open, day and night, to let the sweet air through. I had the same feeling years later when I opened the bedroom windows in her childhood home in Schilpario. The fresh Italian air was just like the breezes that blew off the pristine lakes of Minnesota. I love to leave doors and windows open, too, and I know this came from her example.

That Dress

One summer day, when Lucy was working downstairs in her shop, I went through her closet. I opened the wide door, and the clean scent of lavender and pressed linen greeted me. I don't know what I was looking for, but I liked to snoop. Lucy with the lovely Italian accent had lived a long time, and I was sure she had some artifacts from the past that would be of interest.

Her closet was unlike any others I knew. First of all, it was spacious. And secondly, it wasn't crammed with clothes. Three hatboxes rested neatly on the shelf over the rod. There were two pairs of shoes on the polished floor – one pair of simple black leather pumps, and a pair of embroidered bedroom shoes, piped in black velvet on a cloisonné print in aqua, black, and deep rose. Her third pair of shoes – her work shoes, black leather lace-ups with a two-inch Cuban heel – she was wearing at the moment, down in the shop. I thought it strange that a woman who sold shoes didn't have more of them. When the work shoes wore out, she would order a new pair, but not before she needed them.

As her closet went, spare and practical, so did the rest of the house. In fact, there wasn't any junk in her house at all – no tchotchkes, no clutter whatsoever. She didn't save ribbon and wrapping paper like Viola, and there wasn't a long pole in her closet with a choice of several winter coats to wear. Lucy had *one*. Granted, if you were going to own one proper coat, it should be like hers: navy blue silk wool with wooden buttons, an empire cut, straight sleeves, and a stand-up collar. It was very Givenchy, but it wasn't French; it had been handmade by her in the shop below. She lined it in midnight blue satin, opulent, but no one ever saw the lining. Only Lucy.

The other aspect of her personal closet that amazed me was that she had three identical dresses. They were navy blue silk with white polka dots. Shirtwaist in style, the dress had a notched collar, short sleeves, tiny white pearl buttons, and matching buttonholes on the opposite placket; a nipped waist with a thin belt made from the polka-dot material gave way to a full skirt that was neither busy nor fussy, but draped beautifully and was exactly right. Appropriate.

I was eleven years old, and this trio of identical dresses fascinated me. Lucy had created a uniform for church and social events, in the form of this dress. She would accessorize it differently for various occasions. Sometimes she wore a locket on a long chain, other times a pin at the collar. Often, according to the season, she would wear the dress with a navy blue cashmere cardigan from Italy, which was kept folded in her drawer, without a pull or a stain or a hole. Her only sweater looked new, and I knew she wore it a lot. She took care of everything she owned as though it was irreplaceable.

I went down the stairs to ask her about the dress situation.

Lucy was sewing at her machine. There was a bright work lamp over it, on a snakelike coil. She'd push and pull that lamp around, up, and down to see her stitches in the best light, then move it out of the way (after all, the bulb was bright and hot) when she released the wheel to wind the bobbin.

When she finished a job and stood up, she'd swing out of her rolling stool, with its low back and handmade pillow seat, like a concert pianist who'd just finished a concerto on the stage of Carnegie Hall. She was one with her instrument: the sewing machine.

When I came into the room (and I was so chic at the time – an eleven-year-old with style, wearing a long rope of wooden beads with a navy blue scooter skirt), she looked up at me and smiled. Beamed. Whenever I came into the room, she'd light up, so *happy* to see me. No one ever in the course of my entire life was ever as happy to see me as she was. Looking back, now, I realize that you only ever need one person who lights up that way when you enter a room. One person is all it takes to give a kid confidence.

'Grandma, I have a question. Why don't you have a lot of clothes?'

She smiled. 'I have plenty of clothes.'

'No, you don't. You have three dresses and one coat. And the dresses are all the same. You only have two pair of shoes. Three, if you count those.' I pointed at the plain black leather lace-ups.

'How many dresses should I have?' she asked.

'More than three.'

She laughed. 'How many can I wear at one time?'

'One.' I was no fool. That was an easy question.

'So how many do I need?' she asked.

I thought for a moment. 'Well, I guess the answer is one.'

'So you see, I have too many.'

I had to process this logic. After all, my fashion gene had kicked in, and here, my Lucy was a creator of clothing, she could make anything she imagined. *Anything.* I wanted to see her wearing the goods. And I wanted to see *a lot*. Her simple, straight black skirt and white blouse wasn't enough.

I had seen pictures of the dresses, skirts, blouses, suits, and coats she had made for my mother and her twin sister. I knew Lucy could make evening gowns of chiffon, sundresses of cotton pique with eyelet lace, and eventually an exquisite peau de soie silk wedding gown for my mother, which I was allowed to look at but never touch. The skirt on my mother's wedding gown was a full 360-degree circle skirt with layers of white tulle underneath. Lucy was capable of high fashion. I knew Lucy had chic and cool *in* her, I had *seen* it, so why wasn't she wearing her own couture? I didn't even know how to express this to her; in my mind, it seemed insulting to point out that she didn't have much. So instead I asked, 'Why the polka dots?'

'White polka dots on navy blue are classic. You can wear that fabric to a wedding or a funeral or a party, and it's always just right.'

Years later, when I moved to New York City and was making my living by day as an office temp to finance my theatrical dreams at night, I lived in a boardinghouse. I needed a dress to wear to weddings and funerals and the occasional fancy party (with the dual purpose of making connections and eating enough hors d'oeuvres at Manhattan parties so that I wouldn't have to buy dinner later). 'Beauty on a budget' didn't begin to describe my circumstances. Like every girl without connections that ever moved to New York City to find a job and make a life, I was *broke*. Everything I made went to rent and playwriting. But I needed to look good, to give an impression that I was serious and had taste, and maybe, if there was a miracle to occur, that I was actually going places.

I went to B. Altman's to look for a dress. I scoured the racks. And almost without looking for it, I came upon a navy blue and white polka dot dress with short sleeves, a square collar, covered buttons, and a matching belt. The skirt portion was fitted around the hips and fell into pleats above the knee. It was the 1980s, so it had shoulder pads. At this point in the book, my friends are laughing as they read this, because they know The Dress; they have pictures of me in it, because I wore that dress absolutely *everywhere*, from the Benton/Doughan wedding in Wareham, Massachusetts, to a funeral in lower Manhattan, and every other event I was invited to in between.

I wore it professionally on interviews, and socially to parties, and on days I will never forget, like the autumn day in 1988 when I signed with my first literary agent, the impeccable Wiley Hausam at International Creative Management. Whatever Lucy had wanted to impart to me about sticking with the classics and keeping things simple in the wardrobe department somehow got *in*. When I wanted to jazz up that dress by day, I wore white gloves with it. And when I wore it at night, I'd drape fake pearls like Coco Chanel. Lucy was right. I never had to worry if the dress was appropriate, because it was, and remains ever so.

This effortless style is known as *sprezzatura*. Lucy took it a step further. When you have good taste, and you know what is required, you never need agonize about what to wear. You will hopefully find that one article of clothing that looks good on you, and says who you are, and that's nice. But the important lesson is that having the right dress in your closet means you don't have to waste time shopping incessantly for clothes, buying things you will never wear. The navy and white polka dot dress saves time and money, neither of which should ever be wasted. That dress also made me feel pretty, which is the best reason for wearing it, second only to emulating Lucy, who it seemed, had common sense and good taste, the two characteristics that make an otherwise good woman a lady.

CHAPTER 3

THE FACTORY LIFE

Martins Creek, Pennsylvania, is a small village in the green flats of the northeastern Pennsylvania countryside on the way to Easton, which, along with Allentown and Bethlehem, completes a trio of cities known for steel, manufacturing, and university life (Lafayette, Lehigh, and more).

A few miles down the road from Viola's house, farther still from Roseto, and only seventy miles from New York City, Martins Creek was the perfect location for my grandparents' new factory. It was far enough from the bustle of their friendly competition, and yet had an experienced workforce of machine operators who could cut, assemble, and sew fine blouses for the postwar American woman.

Martins Creek was not unknown to my grandparents. Viola's baby sister Lavinia lived there with her husband and their family, as well as her sister Edith (Ines), who, with her husband, owned and operated an atmospheric Italian restaurant called the Little Venice. It was there, at the bar, that my grandfather first heard of the availability of the

51

empty factory nearby, resulting in their purchase of the building.

Located directly behind the restaurant, past a flat grove of pear trees, was a two-story gray sandstone building on a neat green acre of land. The lower floor would host the cutting room, while the upper floor would be used for assembling, finishing, and shipping.

Garment factories were set in residential neighborhoods in these small manufacturing towns, which was convenient, as women (operators) could walk to work after dropping their children off at school. In the 1940s it was unlikely that a family would have two cars, so the women walked, while their husbands drove to work to the slate quarries, or Bethlehem Steel, or Alpha Cement. The needs of the workforce were considered from the outset by management. Viola knew the key to long-term success was to build a reliable and excellent team, so she put the word out through her known channels in Martins Creek that she and my grandfather were to soon open a mill. The applications poured in as they readied the physical plant.

Own Your Own Business

The entrance to the mill was strictly utilitarian. A set of rough-hewn steps and a potchkied landing made of wide wooden planks with gap-toothed spaces led to a glass door. Inside the door was the clock punch, and off to one side, the office.

Over that entrance, in catchy red and white, was the name of the company: 'The Yolanda Manufacturing Company.' And more to the point, the name of the co-owner, my grandmother. The power of that name, and what that meant in the world, was not lost on the buyers, middlemen, suppliers, or machine operators, or on our family. Viola's given name, Yolanda, defined the endeavor. Viola may have had a maiden name that sounded English, Perin (most Venetian names don't end in vowels), but there was no hiding behind the Anglican sound for her. She was upfront and proud to be Italian American, the daughter of immigrants, from the Veneto.

There was a dividing line between the Italians who changed their names to assimilate in business or fit in socially and the ones who did not. Viola didn't have any patience with faking it. She always felt badly for the Italians who, upon entrance to the United States, had their surnames changed or misspelled by a processing agent.

However, when it came time to put her name on the business, there was no way it would be the Viola Company. The name was my grandfather's idea, and it was, perhaps, the best gift he had ever given his wife. She was proud to give the company the name her immigrant parents had given to her. Viola was also eager, at long last, after years of working for others, to stand behind her brand, determined to deliver a product close to perfect and assume the role of the eight-hundred-pound gorilla to ensure quality control. They opened the mill shortly before Viola's thirty-sixth birthday, in 1943.

Made in the USA

A blouse begins with a sketch that is broken down by piece and via size by measurement. The fabric is purchased by the mill (the price is negotiated), along with the extras: buttons, zippers, piping, specialty collars, embellishments or embroidered insets. All these elements were purchased from salesmen who become an ongoing and important part of the process of manufacturing, an extended family of suppliers, purveyors, and salesmen as familiar to my grandparents as the workers on the plant floor.

The cutting room was on the ground floor of the factory, and the machines, office, finishing, and shipping were on the first floor. The five-foot bolts of fabric were delivered, sealed in plain brown paper casing. The fabric bolt is mounted onto a roller at one end of the table, and then pulled along the length of the table, then rolled out, back and forth, with thin sheets of paper applied between the layers. On top of this layer cake of fabric, thin pattern paper printed in midnight blue ink with the dimensions and parts of a blouse is placed, carefully, to use every inch of fabric and avoid waste. You had to be a bit of an architect when looking at the pattern paper.

Sometimes I could make out collars, or a placket or a sleeve, but most of the time, this massive pattern looked like a map of a world I didn't know.

Over the table, a stainless steel saw with a very thin blade and a cover was pulled down from the ceiling and operated by the cutter. He artfully handled the blade, slicing through the layers of material, following the pattern exactly. The cutter had to be physically strong, have a good sense of concentration, and wield the blade precisely.

Two men called graders would assist him, removing the pieces as they went. This is not a scientific observation, just my own, but I never saw a short man in the job of cutter. The man who handled the blade was always tall and lanky, with long arms.

Upstairs, the main room of the shop was an orderly succession of sewing machines set out in rows on either side of a wide central aisle, attended by small metal stools with low backs. At the end of each row was a large canvas bin on wheels, where the assembled goods were placed, to be taken to finishing, where the sleeves were turned and the blouses pressed, then hung, bagged, or boxed.

Overhead, an elaborate spiderweb of wires provided electricity to run the machines and illuminate the work lamps over the threaders. The bulk of the machines were for sewing, but there were additional models for detail work like button-holing and grommet placement. The sewing machines looked similar – black enamel casing over the curves of the body, spiked by the silver wheel, needle shank, threader, and bobbins – but in time they also assumed the personalities of their operators. Some ladies made cushions for their stools; others organized their tools (short-handled scissors, small screwdrivers) in small boxes or initialed cups. They kept their personal effects in the metal drawers underneath the machines. There was room enough to tuck their purse, lunch, and odds and ends.

At the far end of this large room was a loading dock. A large roll-away door lifted up and out on a track, which turned the back of the factory into an open-air space. A Silver Line tractor trailer would pull right up to the dock, a temporary bridge would be snapped in, and the stock would be loaded on, in bags, ticketed to ship, or on hanging racks on wheels, or folded in boxes individually like unwrapped presents. Due to the volume of goods produced by local factories, the expense of the truck rental was often shared with other mills. These trucks were loaded, then driven into New York City, where the goods were distributed through middlemen in the garment district of midtown.

On days when I would visit the factory with my grandmother, it was usually a weekend, so the mill was empty. Even when the factory was idle, a haze of dust hung in the air from fabric filaments. In bright sunlight, the fabric dust looked like gray snow.

I'd go through the drawers under the sewing

machines to steal chewing gum or bogart a small silver bobbin of hot pink thread while Viola was in the office checking the mail. There were all sorts of things in the operators' drawers – photographs in small leather cases, rosaries, and coins for the soda machine. An old-fashioned refrigerated chest was positioned in the front of the factory loaded with chocolate and orange A-Treat Soda. Viola would often enlist us to tear union labels (ILGWU) off a spool – we were quick with our small hands – to be sewn in the collar of the blouses, or to turn sleeves on finished blouses. If we weren't ripping tickets, she gave us a magnet to collect straight pins from the cracks in the factory floor. We would place the pins in a box, to be reused in the cutting room.

The bins at the end of the aisles were filled with bundles of piecework that the operators would sew together the following week. Fresh from the cutting room, these bundles looked like a stack of puzzle pieces, tied together with streamers of fabric from the edges of the cut fabric.

The wise manufacturer negotiates deals, looks for bargains, and develops a sixth sense for exactly how much trim or how many buttons or zippers are needed on a certain job. It's the salesman's job to suggest options, one button over another or a particular brand of thread. Sometimes my grandfather would buy basics in bulk, knowing that he would need inventory on stock items like small clear buttons for neck loops, or sturdy white or black thread.

All the elements needed to make a blouse factor into the cost for the manufacturer as well as the labor and overhead. My grandparents ran a union shop, so they included pension expenses and fees in their bids. The price of a blouse is negotiated in lots, and the manufacturer is paid for his work by the dozen. It's the job of the manufacturer to negotiate the profit margin.

Viola often worried about 'meeting payroll,' because things can go wrong in the process of garment manufacturing. The mill was responsible for errors. These errors (an uneven stitch, a collar set improperly, a pocket in the wrong place) had to be fixed, and this cost the mill time and money. It was an ongoing challenge to stay in profit. After all, human beings were making the blouses by hand, so you could count on errors. By contrast, you could also count on great artistry and speed, in the hands of experienced operators.

Observing operators working at their machines, heads bowed in concentration as they spin the wheel, guide the fabric through the threader, and pump the pedal, is like watching an orchestra on the stage at Carnegie Hall. There is a syncopation to their movements, and a rhythm to the whole.

In the heyday of production, fifty employees (including cutters, factory floor workers including graders, sample makers, examiners, operators, collar setters, buttonholers, and pressers) assembled the pieces on the machines, which resulted in a finished blouse.

A blouse moved through the operations of the factory from cutting to assembling, to pressing, and on to finishing, where the blouses were hung, ticketed, and bagged, looking as they will when you peruse them on a rack in a department store.

Viola was The Boss. She ensured every blouse that shipped from her mill should be of the highest and best quality. She would not only oversee the work but sit down among the operators, like a pace car on a speedway before a great race, and lead the effort. She led by example, as well as by the following factory rules:

- Hire the best employee.
- Use the specific and special talent of the employee.
- Be able to perform every task that you hire someone else to do.
- Work alongside those you hire; to oversee is not enough.
- Pitch in when there's a deadline.
- If an operator is out, sit down and take her place.
- Have an understanding of the equipment, and how to repair it.
- There is no such thing as a silent partner. When you owe someone money, they own you.
- Do not be smug in success. Stay humble and you'll stay in business for the long run.
- When you take a risk, no second-guessing, no looking back. Plow.

Viola was a tough boss. She was relentless, and told me she made operators cry from time to time. The pressure was on, and everybody felt it; every person had to process that pressure. I think of the operators when I have a deadline. I think of the pressure to be perfect and to work nimbly and quickly when you're tired, or don't feel well, or are distracted by life at home or responsibilities to your family. Like them, I remind myself that I'm doing it for my family – and like them, I focus.

Viola did not coddle, but there was modulated respect when a job was done well. I can see, from the gifts the employees gave my grandparents, that they had respect for them, if not affection. They wrote funny poems upon anniversaries in the mill and on their retirement, but they were never called Viola and Dick. They were Mr and Mrs Trigiani.

Viola's years as a forelady working for Mr Rosenberg helped her develop her managerial style. The output of the factory and the excellence of the product was *her* responsibility. There was no way Viola was going to lose her job or botch an order, so she was a stern taskmaster. Time was not only money; her reputation was on the line. And for Viola, her good reputation and ability to deliver the goods was all they had when my grandfather got on the train in a suit and hat to travel into New York City to find work.

Viola told me that she and Grandpop designed a business plan that they would not vary from in the years that they owned and operated the mill.

My grandfather was the front man. This was a natural position for Grandpop, as he was intelligent, had good taste and was easygoing. He would dress up, go into New York City by train, and meet with various companies in the garment district, where he'd make deals to manufacture blouses, created and sold by the dozen.

As a machinist, my grandfather purchased the equipment and maintained it. He also, according to their partnership contract (they had a very detailed legal agreement between them as full partners), leased the machinery to my grandmother, who owned the building. I learned from them to go to a proper attorney and arrange contracts for any business venture. Further, a proper will saved my grandmother a great deal of anxiety when my grandfather died. Every detail was discussed prior to his death, so Viola had few surprises when tragedy struck.

Yolanda Manufacturing stayed in production fifty weeks a year. The traditional vacation period for the blouse mills was the first two weeks of July. During those weeks, when my grandparents had young children, they went to Atlantic City, to Lake George in upstate New York, or to New England. While they worked hard year-round, when they were off the clock, they relaxed.

Once the operators and suppliers were paid, my grandparents took their cut above the small salaries they pulled from the mill. There were times when they did well, and times when they had to take a lesser deal to keep the factory in operation. Luckily, my grandfather's skill with the machines kept any money that might have gone to repairs in their pockets. He worked in the factory on a daily basis also, but his schedule was more flexible than Viola's. She left before dawn and returned home in time for dinner. He would get the kids off to school and then go to work. The family life thrived around the business.

The mill was an all-consuming, often family-wide venture. Viola would invite her sisters over in a crunch when a deadline was looming. Her children were enlisted to help when the pressure was on. Cousins came through to pitch in. It was natural for Viola to ask for extra hands, as she took the rule of farm life into the factory. If you wanted to eat, you had to work.

When the tough times came, Viola was ready for them because she didn't squander her time and money when the coffers were flush. She told me that when you own your own business, you can never coast, because there is no way to predict what will come. You must rise to meet every challenge, because if you fail, you lose your mill, and the jobs that you provide with it. While the mill employed upward of fifty people, the number grows into the hundreds when you consider the businesses that thrived off the mill. Viola's ledgers are neatly filled with payments to locally owned businesses like the Roseto Paper Box Company, Leader Thread, Fremont Thread, and Silver Line Trucking.

There was a sense of community among her fellow manufacturers, who were also the competition. They knew that the success of their small enterprises extended beyond their profit margins; many families beyond those employed by the mill benefited from this way of life. When a competitor couldn't fulfill an order, he'd swing the work your way. Places like Perfect Shirt often shared an order, thus keeping a workforce active in two mills, both benefiting from the deal.

Yolanda Manufacturing made blouses for Alice Wills Fashions, Dersh Blouse Company, and Lady Helene Blouses, among others. My grandparents' old boss Mr Rosenberg at Bangor Clothing Company threw them a deal here and there. They had put in their years under him, and now he considered them equals, and made sure that opportunities came their way. He recommended Yolanda Manufacturing with the full knowledge that Viola would deliver.

Relationships, Relationships, Relationships

The *schmatte* business, or the rag trade, as it was known then, whose epicenter was in midtown Manhattan, was built on years of relationships, cultivated from the time when my grandparents were young. These alliances and, ultimately, friendships were the fuel that drove the engine of the Yolanda Manufacturing Company. All the years on the floor of the factory mastering new tasks and equipment taught my grandparents everything they needed to know to run their own shop. But, they knew they couldn't do it alone. Relationships would sustain the new operation and help it grow. Loyalty was rewarded. If they liked you in the garment district, they looked out for you, and would recommend you for extra work, or offer you new opportunities that would challenge your work force, and build your business.

In those days (Yolanda Manufacturing was founded in 1943, with the official paperwork of my grandparents' business partnership filed in 1945), most clothes worn in the United States and around the world were made in these small American factories (northeastern Pennsylvania was loaded with them). My grandparents created higher-end blouses sold in department stores by middlemen who also took a cut, many of the designs inspired by fashions worn in the movies. In our current celebrity-driven culture, it's an interesting note that the hunger for Hollywood glamour was key to design, production, and sales even then.

Often a movie star would lend her name to a pattern company, sponsor a fashion line, or let a character she played take the honors to sell a particular garment to the general public. There were varying degrees of participation by the actresses, and their compensation reflected their input and effort. The tags that hung on the blouses featured their glamorous faces, often printed with their signatures. Sometimes their signature was a true endorsement; other times, their image was simply on contractual loan for a set time period, to push ready-made goods to the discerning shopper looking for her own handful of Hollywood stardust.

Viola told me about the various styles of blouses made in their factory, including one that was known as the Gene Tierney, a blouse with a horse embroidered on the pocket, a variation of which was worn by the starlet in a movie. For my grandparents, whose own romance had blossomed in the early 1930s, with dates to Hollywood movies as their favorite pastime, it seemed that things had come full circle. How long would the good times last?

Eventually, ceding to my grandfather's illness, they sold the Yolanda Manufacturing Company in 1967. They had been in business for themselves for twenty-four years. Later, when we talked about the closing of the factory, it was with great sadness on Viola's part. They closed the factory on March 15, 1967. Ironically, one year later to the day, Michael Trigiani died. Viola lost her husband and her factory in close proximity, responding to the loss of both with her typical pluck: she went back to work.

While Viola retired from the Yolanda Manufacturing Company, she did not officially from the workforce. Within a year of my grandfather's death, she found herself back on the machines, subbing as an operator in a friend's blouse mill. She became a factory temp, and loved it. When she reached the age of seventy-two, she was thrilled, because that's the official age when the United States government waives income tax. She could put in an eight-hour day on the machine and keep the tax money. The drive and ambition that had served her all of her working life now came with a bonus at the end, and she reveled in it.

One by one, the bustling, busy, profitable, family-owned factories closed in Northampton County until only a few stalwarts remained through the 1970s, pushing hard, using the old manufacturing model as long as they could, until the work was no longer there. By the mid-1980s, most manufacturing had decamped overseas for cheaper labor and materials. By the early 1990s, most of the mills were closed. The small towns punctuated with mills became bedroom communities as younger generations moved to more populous cities, seeking work.

Today, when you drive through my grandmother's stomping grounds in Pennsylvania, you see the abandoned factories, nestled among weeds, with broken-out windows and empty parking lots. Once-vibrant operations with names like Rose Marie Fashions etched in cursive letters on factory doors are gone. Small business was personal in those days, and often you honored a mother or a daughter by naming the factory after her. The entrance doors painted with signs indicating the operations within: office, cutting room, shipping, have peeled off with age.

The mills that sustained these communities are gone.

When I was in college in the early 1980s, I asked Viola to ask the current owner of her factory building for her sign over the door, which had remained there twenty-five years after she had sold the building. A few months later she gave it to me, rusted, with nail holes in it, but there is no mistaking the original grandeur: in bold white the name of her company, on a field of bright red. You could see the sign from a distance, a poppy against the gray sandstone. 'Why do you want this, Adri?' she asked me. 'I want to remember your mill,' I told her.

The loss of the mill and all it represented was a blow to our family, and by extension, and no less devastatingly, to our country. Here we are, years later, and the effects of the loss remain vivid. Imagine a time when a machinist and a seamstress, one with a sixth-grade education, the other less, could join forces, form a partnership, start their own mill, employ a diligent workforce, and *thrive*.

Imagine a time when you could fulfill a lifelong dream, after years of experience working for others, walk into a bank, and secure a loan to start your own business, building upon the knowledge that comes from making a living from the labor of your own hands.

Imagine a time when you could operate the business, and provide a community with steady jobs, buy a home, and educate your children. My grandparents did all of that, and as a sidebar, they were active in their community. They helped to build a convent for the Salesian nuns and subsequently a school in Roseto, with their fellow Rosetans, who pledged, at that time, a great deal of money, because they believed in education – and put their money where their hearts were. When I read the ledgers now, I am so proud of them. They gave generously to causes they believed in. I never knew the extent of their philanthropy in financial terms until I studied the ledgers, because they never talked about these gifts, but I certainly understood their emotional commitment.

In later years, Viola could not understand how our country would succeed if we weren't supplying our people and the world's people with products we had made here, with our own hands. She knew that her small factory affected hundreds of lives, and the income of countless families, from the machine operator who placed the collar at her station in the mill in Martins Creek to the salesgirl who earned a commission selling that same blouse, off the rack, on the floor of Macy's.

Every stratum of worker benefited from American-made goods. We demonstrated through our own efforts goods of quality, durability, and excellence. As immigrants, we were assured jobs, and once having mastered the skill, we could turn around and teach it to others. We were, in a sense, our product, as we defined it: consistent craftsmanship and excellent results, which meant *American* in the marketplace.

Further, my grandparents were prudent as they set the price of the blouse, knowing that to oversell the goods or undersell them, too, had a ripple effect. The idea was to *stay* in business by offering the best quality for the best price, not to overprice and lose the deal altogether. Short-term greed was never a viable long-term solution in business. The point of going into business was to remain there for many years. This commitment to stability was good for everyone: from the career operator to the summer hire who might go off to college in the fall, with actual experience working a trade under her belt.

Even though my grandmother rose from operator to to owner, her own family and my grandfather's family was populated with union operators who put in thirty years and upward on the machines, providing income for their families. Some were widowed, others provided a second income to their husbands' paychecks. The women I knew growing up worked outside the home, and were proud to do so, year after year. It gave them a sense of accomplishment and sustenance. I never knew anything but working mothers, and was well aware that my mother had a career before she had seven children. It seemed that everyone worked, and that work made life better. It wasn't just about the paycheck – though that was important. A job well done led to a sense of accomplishment and enduring purpose: to feed the family's bottom line.

Child care for working families was a constant part of the discussion, and a priority for my grandmother. Viola would take three years off when my father was born; six years later she took two years off when her twins were born, and only six months when her fourth baby was born, as this was the summer before they opened the Yolanda Manufacturing Company. Years later when she wrote down her story, she remembered these dates clearly. They had been negotiated and discussed within her family. Viola used all avenues of child care available to her – family members (my grandfather's cousin Zizi Mary and others), neighbors, and even nuns.

In 1988, after a slew of office jobs and second jobs to provide additional income, I got my first job writing for television comedies. I saw Viola's factory model in effect in an entirely different venue. A television network, through the support of advertisers, provided programming, hiring writers, directors, producers, actors, stagehands, designers, their crews, down to craft services, the folks who make a wagon of snacks for the actors and crew as they rehearsed to make television shows. Beyond these hires, once the show was made, the ripple effect of jobs extended to the graphic designers, distributors, and local affiliates who were employed and lived off the central idea, that we are making shows here, to entertain and enlighten, but also to advertise products that the audience will buy as a result of viewing the show.

Thousands of families lived off of the creation and distribution of our shows. Soon enough, by the mid-1990s, with cheaper programming (sounds familiar) on the boards and with a restless public clamoring for real-life antics instead of scripted shows, the model sank, and with it quality programming that had been the backbone of network and cable television for years. Some might argue that we deserved to fail – we got too big, or maybe the quality wavered in many instances.

However, we do ourselves no favors when we destroy the ability to provide goods and services to a buyer by overpricing ourselves or undercutting our product with watered-down versions of what we create. And yes, some survive the seismic changes that come with destroying one model in order to create anew, but more often than not, we don't. It is true that we wind up with less product, less shows, and less artisans employed in the long run. We certainly don't survive stronger, with more jobs to offer. We all lose. When the jobs are gone, we have learned the hard way, they are *gone*.

If Viola were young today, she would invent her own new business model and manufacture goods her own way, with a small workforce, providing a niche product to the American consumer. I know it would involve clothing, and that whatever she built would be of excellent quality. There's something wrong when you can buy a new pair of wool pants more cheaply than it costs to dry-clean them. No wonder we buy so much clothing; it isn't built to last, because we don't expect it to. My sisters and I still wear Viola's coats, and imagine, they are over sixty years old. It's called vintage now. I marvel at the seams, the pocket insets, the collars, the lining, the cuffs, the covered buttons – the magnificence of an everyday garment, built American.

CHAPTER 4

STOREFRONT COUTURIER

While Viola's business trajectory went from machine operator to eventual owner, the same was not true for Lucy. She never worked in a factory again after her stint in Hoboken. Instead, she became a storefront couturier, and an alteration seamstress for hire at the local department store.

Lucy preferred creating for the individual client. She never tired of the challenge of one-of-a-kind creations, but she fretted about pleasing her customers. In the custom clothing business, the pressure was as real for Lucy as the factory life was for Viola. A jittery bride could wield as much pressure as a buyer under deadline to deliver goods in the garment district. The stakes may have existed on a different scale, but the anxiety and pressure to please were the same.

Lucy's work was an ever-changing landscape, depending upon who walked into her shop. She had a stable of regular customers, for whom she regularly built skirts, blouses, dresses, and coats. Lucy handled all kinds of fabric, from the most sumptuous to the washable and workable.

She used her basic knowledge to adapt to current trends but gently guided her customers back to classic shapes and styles. She enjoyed making the customer happy and witnessing the transformation of a customer who would try on the garment in the final fitting, and turn to Lucy, thrilled with the results. Lucy never missed the rote sewing that she had done as a machine operator in Hoboken. A custom seamstress, a couturier, was free to be original and manage her own time.

It was so much fun to be with Lucy while she worked. Like Viola, Lucy would give me a magnet to collect pins from the cracks in the floor, or keep me busy sorting buttons from her button box. When Lucy tried to teach me how to sew, I was lousy at it. I don't know if I didn't have the patience, or that it was as simple as a preference for the outdoors, but it soon became clear that I wasn't going to be a seamstress, even an amateur one. If she was displeased with my lack of focus, she never let on. I may not have learned how to build a garment, but the things she taught me in her workroom apply to any creative endeavor. It begins by choosing the best possible elements.

Choose the best fabric.

The differences between burlap and velvet, satin and denim, corduroy and silk, are obvious to the touch. It is also apparent that particular fabrics suit certain clothes created for different occasions.

So, to begin, fabric creates a context for a creation. Fabric indicates where you'll wear the clothing, whether it's day or night, formal or sporty, to witness a sacrament or attend a fish fry. Fabric also says what colors you love to wear, and what textures appeal to you against your skin. Fabric is about climate and season, covering up, or exposing, movement and carriage. Fabric acknowledges your station in life and what you think you deserve, whether you are handmaiden or queen, farmer or land baron.

For Lucy, there was only one choice: you should have the *best*, whether the end result was work overalls or an evening gown. Satin *façonné* should be worn by the village bride, so the gown might last for generations to come. The factory worker should wear a cashmere sweater in the drafty mill, because it's the wool of the highest quality, and therefore it lasts. Cashmere is also durable, and the most comfortable wool against the skin; it adapts in fluctuating temperatures, and does not pill. A child should wear brushed corduroy coveralls, because it's the most sturdy material, a washable cotton that holds color through the hand-me-down chain.

A fine-gauge cotton is easier to press, a strong silk holds its shape, a thick velvet is sumptuous and also warm. Lucy believed if you used the best material, the garment would make a statement. Choose the best fabric once, and you've chosen quality, and therefore simplicity. No need to shop and buy ten items, when one beautifully built garment made of the finest fabric would serve your purpose and have you look forward to wearing it. Lucy thought the most deserving of elegance were the folks who provided it. Nothing made her happier than to build a beautiful garment for a woman who would appreciate it, someone like her, a working woman.

> Nobody has to see how many times you rip out the hem.

There isn't a workday that goes by that I don't consider this bit of wisdom. Lucy ripped out hems, over and over again, until the seams were straight and perfect. She spent hours draping fabric to show off its texture and create the perfect shape. Each fitting improved the garment, and Lucy would not rest until she was satisfied with every stitch. Details mattered.

The results of your hard work should appear effortless. The most glorious creations seem to appear in full out of nowhere. That's the sign of a craftsman. Creating something from nothing is a triumph of imagination and skill. When you sew a stitch, it should be so small that it disappears into the fabric, and becomes part of the whole. The smaller the stitch, the better the seamstress. I imagine words in a novel like stitches. Words should flow seamlessly, without a tug or a pull to take you out of the thought itself.

Aim for *sprezzatura*, elegance that is neither forced nor dictated, that comes from within, effortlessly like zippy dialogue, and is an extension of the person, not words for the sake of them. Description, like sartorial details, should inspire a mood – the way a covered button blends into a coat, never breaking the line, or by contrast how a brass button on the same coat turns it into a uniform. The smallest details make a difference. They change the message.

> Once you cut the pattern, do not stop until you've sewn the last seam.

There are all kinds of seamstresses, as there are levels of craft in every profession. Some seamstresses like to have several projects going at once. They cut several patterns, stack them up, then plow through them, assembling them on the machine. Not so for Lucy. She cut one pattern at a time and then would sew until the garment was complete. Lucy did not rest until a particular garment was finished, every seam perfect, pressed and steamed on the hanger, ready for the customer. Then, she'd start the process all over again with the next job.

Lucy finished what she started. She liked to work methodically, without the distraction of the next job tugging for her attention. Chaos was for the circus. Three rings of action with trapeze artists flipping overhead might be entertaining, but it didn't get the job done. The execution of a good design takes focus and concentration. It may be easier to cut a pile of patterns first, and then sit for long stretches and sew, but Lucy was having none of it. When I asked her why, she told me that she could not do her best unless she focused on one garment at a time. She felt a sense of completion when the job was done from start to finish. She was satisfied when the customer came to pick up her garment, tried it on, and was pleased with the fit. The thrill of being done never left her.

As much as I juggle projects day to day, I never work on two projects simultaneously. I finish one project before starting a new one. There is nothing more exciting than finishing, except the day when a brand new project begins. As Lucy laid out the fabric on the cutting table and pinned the pattern to the material, so it is when I start a new writing project. I surround myself with the elements of the subject I plan to write about: maps, letters, postcards, swatches, tools, photographs – all manner of research clutter my desk to inspire me as I go. Like pattern pieces, small bits of dialogue, stretches of description, are woven together that will eventually become part of the whole. Writing is, in a sense, sewing, and description is the overlay of embroidery that gives a sense of movement and scope, style and distinction.

People remember details more than the dress.

Lucy's goal was to provide simple elegance. She was curious about what was in style, and would cherry-pick ideas from popular trends, but only if those ideas served the customer and the overall design of the garment she was making for her.

Lucy was interested in new ideas and different techniques that might make her garments more beautiful. But she also knew that honing skills she already possessed would make her work better. Lucy believed in multiple fittings, because then she could see her work on the customer and make adjustments. Proper fit was more important than executing the latest style of sleeves. Lucy did not believe in cluttering a garment with extraneous ruffles, bows, pleats, and piping. She believed tacked-on adornments gave a garment a home-made look. Instead, she worked with the grain of the fabric, ruching for texture, and used inventive techniques like attaching a single layer of tulle under the hem of cotton pique to frame the skirt. Lucy's combinations were often surprising – seer-sucker with a trim of striped ticking, or a floral chintz placket on denim coveralls. She knew whimsy, and occasionally indulged in it; but for the most part, what you got when you went to Lucy was classic styling.

I think of her devotion to technique, and how it's the basics to which an artist returns, time and time again. Simple technique serves the artist and the creation by providing a foundation upon which the art is made. For the writer, this is the central idea upon which a story is written. Every day, I ask myself as I work, 'What am I trying to say?'

Lucy asked that same question, in her fashion: 'What am I trying to build?' Technique provides the way to the answer. Restraint is a goal born of precision.

> Wear what you like, not what looks
> good on someone else.

Lucy believed that excessive shopping was a sign of a person who had no idea what looked good on her. Somehow, the sea of choice was supposed to bring a customer closer to knowing what she was looking for, but Lucy knew better.

Lucy thought it was better to make a list of what you love to wear. Begin with styles you have worn and loved. Remember moments when you felt your best, and gravitate back to those styles to winnow down your preferences. Too often we are influenced by trends, or the opinions of others, when really all we need do is wear what we like. Trust who you are, know what you like, and the choices will be clear. You will never be mired in the mud of trends or distracted when you keep the basics in mind. At the end of your search, you'll find you have less clothes, but exactly what you need and will enjoy wearing.

I learned the importance of a uniform from Lucy. I travel, and therefore I need well-made clothing that doesn't wrinkle or bind. As a mother, I don't have a lot of time to think about what I'm going to wear, and as a woman, I don't want to spend a lot of time worrying whether I look appropriate. I admire beautiful fabrics and architectural styling. Simplicity is a lesson I learned from Lucy, and it's a lesson I continue to learn as I go through life.

> When it comes to clothing, the face is
> the most important feature.

Of all the things I appreciated about Lucy's skills as a seamstress, I marveled the most at her collars. Collars serve the same function on a garment as a frame surrounding a painting. The placement, arc, and curve of the neckline frame the face and provide an overall sense of proportion and line to the garment, to emphasize a woman's most important aspect: the face that presents her to the world.

Lucy often made generous collars, which appeared opulent, whether on a coat or dress. Lucy often lined coats with a bright satin, so a rich shot of color peeked out from a sturdy wool.

Lucy believed accessories should mirror the simple lines of a garment. A thin, long chain with a locket worn with a square collar looks prim, yet artful. A lustrous roll collar on a simple A-line coat gives movement and swing to soft wool. A layer of chiffon over a straight silk chemise lends an ethereal mood. No one element should ever throw off another; rather, they should work together in harmony. Simplicity, clean lines, and a clean silhouette work on every age and every figure.

Lucy built clothes for children to ladies of a

certain age, so her acumen and experience making clothing for women was extensive. Throughout her career, she built upon her basic principles, therefore her work was never out of style, never felt antiquated – the emphasis was on the person wearing her creations, not the clothes themselves.

I try to be simple, but like the Italian/Latina girls that ride the B train, I love hoops, chunky jewelry, and bold statement pieces. I like a lot of shine. Here, I may seem to part company with Lucy, but not for long. I often look at the mass of necklaces around my neck and eventually, before I leave the house, remove one or two, knowing that overkill is the opposite of restraint. The effect should never be cluttered or maddening, but tasteful, and hopefully fun.

Make it by hand, and it will last forever.

There is something about a garment made just for you that takes an article of clothing from merely pleasing to the heights of true art. This custom creation doesn't have to be a couture ball gown made from hand-embroidered silk, or any number of ensembles for fancy occasions, it can simply be the most comfortable pajamas you've ever worn.

When Lucy made me pajamas, she chose an antique floral pattern. My favorite set was made of one hundred percent cotton with a small forest green floral, with alternating ticking stripes and strips of flowers. You could easily use this same fabric to make bed linens, napkins, or a parasol.

Lucy knew, by sight, how to fit your pajamas to you. The neck was round, lined, and lay flat. She left extra room in the short puffed sleeve; the bodice flared out and stood away from the waist of the pant. The top never wrinkled or looked sloppy. The pants had wide, straight legs, and the waistband was elastic, covered in the fabric and tacked so it never bound or rolled over. When you put the pajamas on, there was no aspect to them that was uncomfortable, itchy, or tugged. When you slept, they moved with you, weightless and adaptable. The pajamas were so simple, so beautiful, that I easily could have worn them out in public, and they would have looked like a 1970s playsuit.

The greatest lesson of my grandmother's skill as a couturier was her *intent*. From her, I learned that if art is made with love, from the heart, to please someone, it will be treasured, passed down, and remembered. I think of my reader when I write, as Lucy thought about her customer when she built a dress for a special occasion, or her granddaughter, thousands of miles away, sleeping in the pajamas made just for her.

Lucy imagined the customer wearing the dress, and the impact she would make when she entered the room. I imagine the serenity I feel when I read a book that moves me, and I'm introduced into a world that I want to stay in until the story is told.

The power of a garment reinventing the woman is the exact feeling I attempt to create with a story. I hope my reader is inspired to feel the possibilities of love and life through a story or finding, in the character's experience, a new way of looking at things. I hope you will feel better, uplifted, and your best, after you've read a story I have written, just as Lucy hoped a customer felt when she wore a custom dress or coat. When you walked out into the world in a creation by Lucy Bonicelli, you had a certain sense about yourself. Maybe you carried yourself differently, with a sense of pride and possibility. I hope you feel the same, when you read one of my novels. Art makes the spirit soar. And when the spirit is lifted, life follows.

CHAPTER 5

SECURITY

Whenever I spent time in Viola's home in Pennsylvania, I spent a lot of time reading. (You cherished that delicious downtime from the chores.) Among the Literary Guild oeuvre of romantic novels and biographies left by the former owner were self help books published during the Great Depression that caught my attention: *The Magic of Belief* in a plain black leather binding, no dust jacket, and *Think and Grow Rich*, again no dust jacket but a brown leather cover embossed with a top hat, stack of gold coins, and a pair of men's formal evening gloves. Further, a practical guide to life published in the 1950s called *How to Live 365 Days a Year* with a bright red and white jacket that shouted 'Read me!' was stacked with the others on the shelf.

There was also a how-to book written in the late 1940s, the paperback *How to Win Friends and Influence People*, with a bespectacled author Dale Carnegie on the back jacket. These books were read, obviously, time and time again, evident from the loose bindings and dog-eared or bookmarked pages.

When I asked my grandmother about these books, she told me they belonged to my grandfather. The themes were centered on one idea: how to manifest personal success by harnessing the power of your subconscious mind to visualize your goal and get the result you want. The reader, through his own determination and mind control, could attract wealth, shape his financial destiny, and therefore achieve personal happiness. This all sounds very dreamy, and it was – here was a philosophical approach to life that required belief followed by action.

I imagined my grandfather, hat in hand, going from buyer to buyer in the garment district, using the tips in Dr Carnegie's book to score an order for the Yolanda Manufacturing Company. I conjured Viola at sixteen, walking the floors of the Bangor Clothing Company, imagining herself with a desk in the front office, as detailed in the exercises in *The Magic of Belief*.

There was no prestigious college degree, impressive business school master's degree, or family connections that either of my grandmothers or grandfathers could rely upon as a calling card to attract business. They had nothing to recommend them but their experience and desire to lead. They had to invent their own financial philosophy and life plan. They also had to *see* their goal to eventually achieve it. They had to imagine the building, the workforce, the operation itself. They had to think big when ideas were all they owned. They stuck to the tenets of visualization, which is to picture the goal repeatedly, then take the steps to see it through to completion. They did not rest until the factory in their mind's eye was in full operation in Martins Creek. *Think and Grow Rich* contained aspirational advice with specific steps to wealth: how to take the thoughts in your head and turn them into cash.

Viola taught me to save, and the time value of money.

The first rule of savings is sacrifice. I couldn't have everything I wanted, when I wanted it. Viola said, You know what you earned each week. You know exactly what your basic expenditures are, then factor in your debt. First, before you pay any bill, pay yourself. Whether it's five dollars, or fifty or five hundred, secure an account and begin putting money in it today.

Viola and Michael were big on taking the savings and buying government bonds. They were big supporters of bond sales during World War II, and these purchases were the backbone of their personal savings.

They believed in saving money that you will not touch for years. 'Forget it's there!' Viola used to say. That money will accrue interest, no matter how meager, and provide you with a return on your savings. Viola taught me that the road to wealth is making saving money a *habit*. Once you get into the habit, and the earlier you start the process the better, your savings will grow, and as they grow, so will your sense of security and your ability to take a risk. If you want to take a year off, for example, you need to save two years of salary. You'd be surprised, with the occasional windfall and extra paycheck, how you can make money work for you.

Before I left temping as a secretary, I squirreled away enough cash to get me through several months, which led to my first job writing in television. To this day, I have the habit of saving for particular things, and depriving myself of silly expenditures in the face of one wonderful thing. And there have been times in my life when that one wonderful thing was a medical emergency or the need for an unexpected plane ticket.

Buy a home.

Lucy, widowed at the age of thirty-five, was in an entirely different financial situation from Viola. Lucy didn't have a life partner to share the dream or the work to secure the purchase of a home. While her husband was a veteran of World War I, Lucy received no restitution, even though the cancer that killed him was from mustard gas dropped on his platoon in World War I. Lucy did not look for windfalls, or miracle money, nor did she expect her family in Italy to bear the responsibility of helping with her family. With her youth, skill, and vision, she figured it out. She knew she had to invent a plan and, with meager savings and the loss of my grandfather's income from his shoe shop, build a new life alone.

Lucy was living with her three children in the brick building on 5 West Lake Street in Chisholm. She was renting, but did not own it. The same tentacles of the horrors of the Great Depression had reached her mining town, and she could see that things would eventually get better, but not any time soon. In a bold move, she went to a wealthy Italian man (he owned several successful restaurants) who had emigrated from Bergamo (so she shared his background) and asked for a loan to buy her building. This man, Gildo Salvi, cut Lucy a good deal. Within five years of my grandfather's death, and on Lucy's fortieth birthday, she owned her building outright. She told me that every night when she went to sleep, she imagined owning the building. And payment by monthly payment, scraping here and skimping there, she made the payments on a timely basis and paid back the loan. Like Viola, Lucy used visualization as a tool to meet her goal.

Lucy never forgot the generosity of Gildo Salvi, and would often repeat his name to me. On the day of her last payment, Lucy delivered it in person. Mr Salvi told Lucy that he had never expected her to honor the debt in its entirety. He knew of her circumstances, and figured he was doing a good deed, and that was repayment enough. Lucy said, 'You don't know me, Gildo. I could not rest until I paid this debt.'

Lucy credits this act of generosity from Mr Salvi to her family as a solid indication that help was there if you needed it, but if you took that help, the responsibility to pay back the debt was a vow not to be broken. She told me the happiest day of her life was the day she handed Mr Salvi the final payment on the building. She had done it – on her own, dollar by dollar, with the satisfaction of this note, made the future of her family's home secure forever. Lucy now could focus her energy on maintaining the building, providing for her family, and saving for the education of her children.

When it came time for my husband and me to buy our home, I realized that I had an issue.

I don't know how to buy real estate devoid of emotion, because land, houses, yards, and gardens are where a family thrives. Houses hold memories and the fascinating stuff that defines the taste of the occupants. I think of Viola's cluster of Murano glass grapes and Lucy's striped leather ottoman when I think of them. Forgive me, as a smart banker or perceptive broker will tell you *not* to do as I have done. I worked at first to survive, and then to build a family, and now I work to maintain my family. Luckily, I am half of a team with my husband, but I think of Lucy and how circumstances can change in a moment. I live in a state of preparedness for the worst.

Money and emotions are more closely tied than we know. When you buy your first home, make your *love* of it one of the reasons for buying it. The sting of paying off the bank won't hurt as much, when you look at it positively. If your goal is to build a happy life, you will attract the money you need to maintain it because you will work harder to hold on. A home that *you* own will bring your family years of happy memories, and a place where you can wander without shoes – my definition of happiness.

Keep meticulous records.

Every once in a while, I take Viola's work ledgers out of the closet. I like to look at the neat Palmer Method penmanship in fountain-pen ink (midnight blue), chronicling the salaries of the employees and the expenditures of the Yolanda Manufacturing Company. (Did everyone born before 1950 have exquisite handwriting, or is that just me?)

I like to peruse the list of names of the employees and their salaries, written on thin blue lines. There are margin notations of payouts to suppliers. There are comments about unexpected expenses, like a shipping payment that was tacked on, or an extra ten dozen high-end hangers that were not included in the supply order.

Meticulous record keeping is the sign of a serious business. No matter how small your business is, whether you are a one-man operation or you work for a corporation, records are key to understanding what is going out and what is coming in and the labor required to fulfill the obligations of the company. Account for every penny on paper. There is no delusion in numbers. Viola said, keep illusion on the screen at the local movie house; in life, face the facts. Live the factory life in all aspects of living: put one foot in front of the other, one deal at a time, and soon, stitch by stitch, order by order, blouse by blouse, payroll will be met. And after payroll comes profit. And when you get paid, pay yourself first.

Viola worked in extras in her budget. There were allowances for the car, Grandpop's 16mm movie camera habit, and Viola's hat addiction. However, there was no hiding the numbers or manipulating them to put anyone's mind at ease temporarily. Building wealth takes a plan, an honest and ongoing assessment of expenditures and sacrifice. Treat yourself, Viola believed, but never go into debt doing so.

Say no to credit cards.

Banks make fortunes off of credit cards, off of *you* and me. Credit cards were anathema to Lucy and to Viola. By the time I graduated college in the 1980s, there I was, without a job or savings, and I was deluged with offers of free money in the form of credit cards. In my youth, the cards were tempting, and there came a time when I used them to temporarily make ends meet, but I always paid them off on time. When I look back now on the high interest rates that I paid, I wish I had saved the money I gave to the banks.

When I veered off course financially, and lots of us do, I soon turned it around. In 1983, at the behest of a brilliant Merrill Lynch money manager, Tom Sullivan, I bought $500 worth of bonds. Today, that investment is worth over $5,000, and I cannot touch it until my retirement. It pained me to give Tom the money to invest then, and through the years, I wanted to cash it in. I'm so glad I didn't, because it reminds me that even when I had nothing, I saved. Not only must you *live* on what you earn, you have to *save* on what you earn. The sooner you begin saving, the sooner you stop losing sleep over money.

A Marriage Proposal and a Partnership

Michael asked Viola to go for a drive at lunch one day. He took her to 37 Dewey Street in Roseto, Pennsylvania, and parked the car in front of a double red brick home with a green awning, and a long backyard suitable for growing a garden and hanging the wash. Viola took in the charming house on the wide street, and loved it on sight.

The front porch was lovely, with furniture and flower baskets hanging from hooks. Sitting in the car, my grandmother could imagine their future. This house was a few miles from her father's farm, and a block from the Trigiani family homestead on Garibaldi Avenue. Yet there was a sense of privacy on this lovely side street that curved off of Garibaldi. It seemed to Viola like its own world, one that she would like to be a part of.

Viola admitted that a proposal from my grandfather was her highest romantic dream. She worried that my grandfather might not choose her. From the time they met, she chose him, even though she had a nice beau at the time. The nice beau, whom she called 'the Sheik,' did not pass muster with my great-grandfather, as the fellow was flashy, and my practical Nono (as we called him) did not understand how this debonair suitor made his living.

Viola listened to her father. She respected him and, in her way, adored him. He was dear and kind, and a dead ringer for Gepetto as described in the *Pinocchio* story. But for sure, my great-grandfather wasn't going to offer up his firstborn to a less than wonderful man. So, Nono went to the local priest.

If becoming a success in business was Viola's first resolve, her second was to earn her salvation into heaven following the rules of her Roman Catholic religion. If the priest advised my grandmother on any matter, she heeded it. Her wise father knew this, and his plan worked. Viola broke up with Mr Snazzy and turned her attention to my grandfather, by all accounts a catch, and a handsome, good-natured guy.

As they swerved and curved in their unlikely romance, Michael left for a time to work in the

94

Bronx, in New York, and then to East Norwalk, Connecticut. I never asked him, as I was so young when he died, why he left Viola behind after meeting her, and there are no clues in his correspondence. I imagine he had his own brand of wanderlust and wasn't ready to settle down. There are letters, and entries in Viola's diary that tell me their love was a struggle.

Sometimes the goal of marriage seemed impossible to Viola, until the day that they took this drive. My grandfather said the magic words in his proposal of marriage: 'I was thinking we should buy this house. What do you think, Viola?' She told me that moment changed everything. She knew then how much he loved her; in his query was the meaning. Michael Anthony Trigiani wanted to spend the rest of his life with Viola Perin.

This house would be their home.

As soon as my grandmother said yes, and they were married, they went to the bank, and secured the mortgage. My grandmother spent the next fifteen years in her home going to bed each night with the same visual in her head: that of the mortgage contract to the house burning. Viola would focus on this picture until she had paid off the bank and owned their home outright. Every business decision that she made, every dollar that went in the bank, was to pay down that mortgage and eventually to pay it off entirely.

My grandfather believed in borrowing money, and Viola, in paying it off. Their partnership was evenly balanced in this regard, one side fueling the other to success. Viola told me that marriage was a great invention, because built into the contract is a business deal. There is a checks and balances system in place, if both partners agree to use it. When my grandfather ran the numbers, Viola would check them. When Viola had an idea in the mill, she always ran it by my grandfather. They took their partnership seriously. They went to a proper lawyer to make their contracts. They did not rush the process; they pored over evey detail until both were satisfied with every clause and sentence. The partnership contracts for their mill took them three years to negotiate. At this time, they were married for ten years and had four children. Cautious does not begin to describe their approach to business.

Owning your home takes a leap of faith. Choose what you can afford and what you are certain you can maintain. The current obsession with huge homes with enormous rooms and bathrooms, brand-new, custom built, would seem crazy to my grandmothers. Any home can be a palace, if you don't walk the floors at night worried about how to pay for it.

It isn't square footage that creates opulence; it's peace, calm, and the comforting knowledge that we can live well within our means that give us security. It would never have occurred to my grandparents to live in a home that they could not afford. A palace ceases to be home when it empties your peace of mind along with your wallet. Your home should not be about status, but about serenity.

Buying a home was the basis of my grandparents' overall financial plan. When they moved from Dewey Street to outside of town, they were happy, but the mood was bittersweet. Success bought them their home in the country, but nothing would ever be as sweet as the goal of owning their first home, and the proposal that made the dream come true. Years later, Viola would take the turn off Garibaldi to pass their first home at 37 Dewey Street. She missed it for the rest of her life.

Invest in the stock market.

Viola was encouraged to invest in the stock market by her husband, who with a sixth-grade education had risen in esteem in the community as a businessman, becoming a member of the board of directors of the First National Bank in Bangor, Pennsylvania.

It was a very progressive notion to convince freshly minted Italian Americans to put money in a bank. They were highly suspicious of entrusting anyone with their money, and especially not a corporation in the business of making money. But Viola and Michael not only believed in banks, they put every cent they made into them. There was no mattress with cash, or hidden assets in the wall. For a couple of kids born at the turn of the twentieth century, they were practically financial renegades.

Early on, with very few dollars, they began to invest and follow the stock market. Viola used to have me read the stock pages aloud to her from the newspaper as she made lunch. I never liked to deliver bad news, but when a stock was down, and I duly reported the information, she'd have a few curse words for the *Wall Street Journal.*

Upon Viola's death, her portfolio included mainly bluechip stocks in companies that she had a direct understanding of, and whose products she felt an affinity for. The diehards included food companies, energy industries, and the neverfail (!) banking industry. She had managed to hold on to her stock portfolio until her death without raiding it to live. She promised herself that she would live in her home until she died. She visualized that goal also, and made it happen.

Start working early and never, ever retire.

Viola earned her first paycheck at the age of fourteen for 60 cents a week, while Lucy earned her first paycheck at the age of seventeen earning two dollars a week. They started working early, and began to save young. They never blew a paycheck, nor were in the position, by their own spending, to be living hand-to-mouth. They encouraged me to do the same.

Like Viola, Lucy never officially retired. She died on the eve of her ninety-ninth birthday, in a stroke rehabilitation/assisted living hospital. Her hope was to return home, to her life and her shop on West Lake Street. Alas, she never did, but in that time, she never officially closed her shop, or moved from her home. It stood empty, and when I visited her, I would stay there.

Viola sold her factory building a year after my grandfather's death. She did not sell the name outright, but liquidated the contents of the mill, the machinery, the remnants of supplies, and the cutting table.

Viola had now, late in life, a fourth career arc. After working as an operator for hire, then a fore-lady, and then owning and operating her own business, Viola returned to the mill as a machine operator. She took deep satisfaction from staying in the game. She believed retirement happened when they lowered you into the ground. So Viola officially stopped working in April 1997, when she returned to the Heavenly Father.

If, God willing, I live long and productively like my grandmothers, and fellow authors such as Mary Higgins Clark and Maeve Binchy, while maintaining strength of body, mind, and a can-do spirit, I plan on never, ever, ever retiring. This is one instance where I can say *never*. I learned from Lucy and Viola that if you stay in the game and out in the world, there are new things to learn and savor in the final years of life. I plan to hold on to that philosophy until they wrestle the pencil out of my hands.

It takes more than one job to make a living.

Lucy was flexible when it came to taking on extra work. She looked at these short-term jobs as a way to make extra money and expand her skill set.

I try to take on any job offered me if there is a way that I can fulfill the obligations to the boss's (producer or publisher) satisfaction. I learn so much when I take on extra work. I meet new people, develop new alliances, and am introduced to new and often better techniques. Sometimes, a side job will encourage new ways of thinking, or a new approach to my work. The additional compensation can go to pay down the mortgage, or provide a budget for a research trip that leads to more work. You never know. So if it doesn't kill you, do it.

Plan on the rainy day.

The rainy day wasn't a cautionary lyric in a Sinatra song for Lucy and Viola; the wolf was at the door, and he was howling. It wasn't a matter of whether a rainy day was coming, it was a certainty: so be *aware* and be *prepared*.

Lucy's worries were centered around the fear that she had no family in this country, and therefore there was no safety net for her children if something bad happened to her. In a sense, Lucy willed her good health and long life, in order to take care of her family. She took care of her health, knowing that if she got sick, the entire structure of the family and the security of her children would be in jeopardy.

Lucy never complained about her obligations, and while she loved to laugh, listen to opera and read beefy romance novels in Italian, she was thoughtful and private. She appeared, to outsiders, to be stoic and unflappable. But she assured me that there were many nights when she was afraid, and her obligations were so overwhelming, she would give in to her emotions and cry, covering her sobs so her children wouldn't hear her. I don't know what kind of a woman my grandmother would have been had her husband lived and realized his dream of becoming a shoe designer, but I imagine, with his gregarious nature, in success, she would have been more carefree.

Viola, who experienced a level of prosperity, had a different view. She could make the occasional frivolous purchase, and aspire beyond her humble beginnings on the farm, knowing that her partnership with my grandfather would protect her.

Viola worried about overindulging her children because she had a career. Unlike her childhood friends, who worked as operators, or were exclusively homemakers, she was the Boss, and was burdened with the responsibility of running the mill.

At the end of a working day, she did not walk away from it. The kind of ambition Viola had in the 1930s and 1940s was the stuff of shop girl storylines in Hollywood movies. She encountered her share of detractors, but nothing mattered to her as much as the dictates of her own conscience. She was proud to work outside her home, and would not have chosen otherwise.

Lucy was handed her circumstances not by choice but by fate. But I imagine that Lucy's diligence and craftsmanship would have been there, regardless of the level of success and support she had from Carlo. She was also intent on working, because her craft added dimension and purpose to her life.

When my mother married, she gave up her career. My parents married in the late 1950s, and that was the expectation. Now, whether my mother suffered because of this is another story entirely. I knew from the time that I was small that my grandmothers ran their own shows. I felt sorry for my beautiful mother that she hadn't been able to work after she had our family. But as it turns out, my generation is back to basics, surviving like our grandmothers, fending off the wolf at the door.

CHAPTER 6

LA BELLA FIGURA

The Basics

Viola established a beauty routine and a look that was simple. She wore cherries in the snow lipstick, Arpège perfume, and a hat in the sun. Her skin creams were strictly Estée Lauder because she appreciated the free gift with purchase. Her sister Helen, the hairdresser, gave her the latest medium cuts for wavy hair, through 1980. Then Viola went with the modified Betty White: height on top, loose waves to the side, fringe of curls in a flip.

Lucy used a face cream, powder, and a little rouge from time to time. I don't know what they would make of my tackle box of cosmetics, but whatever I do, I do in the hopes of looking like my grandmothers.

Begin each day in a state of calm.

Lucy taught me to begin each day in a state of calm.

In Lucy's home, you did not wake up to alarms,

chaos, arguments, and noise. Lucy rose an hour before her children, put on her coffee, ate her breakfast, and read her papers, and by the time the children were up, she was ready to help them get up and out the door.

Eat a good breakfast.

The small act of rising early and eating breakfast will make a big difference in your state of mind as you face the workday. When we take advantage of the early hours of the morning, we have a chance to think and prepare for our day. Once everyone is up, the day takes off and almost runs away from you. Here, in the serenity of early morning, you can take time for yourself and your thoughts. I read the papers, check my calendar, and read something for pleasure. I prepare my breakfast, Viola style.

Every morning, Viola prepared her version of a latté, a bowl of steamed milk with half a cup of strong coffee in it. Viola added sugar, and then would take the heel of the bread from the day before and dip it into the milk and coffee. Sometimes she'd break up crackers in the milk instead of the heel of the bread. I substitute whole wheat toast with peanut butter, or I have an egg with the latté.

The very act of holding the warm, oversize ceramic cup in a big easy chair in the quiet of the morning begins my day with a ritual that reminds me of the women that came before me.

Lucy's breakfast routine included a poached egg,

toast, and freshly squeezed orange juice. She had an old-fashioned juice squeezer, and she made the juice fresh, as you sat down. She too, steamed milk and put a few tablespoons of fresh-brewed coffee in (yes, I was eleven) with a little sugar. She would have black coffee, juice, and an egg.

Lucy's newspapers were on the table. She read *Corriere della Sera*, the Italian newspaper published in the States, *L'Eco di Bergamo* from back home in Italy, and of course the *Chisholm Free Press*, edited by her longtime friend Veda Ponikvar.

Lucy had a deep interest in politics. She was a lifelong Democrat and kept up on current events in this country and in Italy. She had lived in Italy as the roots of fascism were taking hold, and therefore had strong opinions about democracy.

Viola read the *Easton Express* and the *Wall Street Journal*. When she was a girl, her family were also Democrats, but when she married, she became a Republican, like her husband. In the 1930s, Italian Americans were just getting a foothold in local politics and business, and my grandfather liked the Republican take on small government. He eventually ran for chief burgess (mayor) of Roseto and won. Viola dutifully ran the women's Republican club in the early to mid-1930s.

There is no beauty without intelligence.

Breakfast, politics, reading the newspapers, and being involved in local government may seem at odds with the attributes that create La Bella Figura. For Viola and Lucy, feminine beauty was first and foremost about intelligence. 'Nobody likes a pretty dope,' Viola once said. 'No matter *how* pretty she is.'

Informed opinions, the ability to participate in intelligent conversation, and a personal point of view made a woman *interesting*, and therefore attractive. Perhaps also, because both of my grandmothers held education in the highest regard, and they were unable to complete their own, they were hungry for information. They were self-educated, so a big component of their ongoing education was staying current. Viola kept the addresses of her congressmen and senators in her phone book, and when she wanted her opinion known, she would write to them.

Beauty by definition was more than a combination of admirable physical attributes and a dazzling smile. Beauty was a greater ideal that encompassed awareness and ambition. If self-esteem is rooted in pride in one's accomplishments, my grandmothers knew that no goal could be achieved without the development of a keen and curious mind. It wasn't enough to have a pretty face, you had to have the smarts to back it up. And if you had the smarts, you'd better use them.

Purpose made my grandmothers attractive. Their ability to take care of themselves financially, to live alone happily, and to continue to work long after retirement age gave them energy and confidence.

Nothing was more important to Viola and Lucy than to be independent and make their own decisions. They had opinions. Work kept them out in the world, connecting with people of all ages, it also kept them in the moment, and gave them a world view. The scope of their lives did not become narrow as they aged, it grew wider. And now, they had acquired wisdom so they had greater gifts to share. They weren't consumed with worry about how they looked, because they were busy, *living*, participating fully in the world around them.

Widen your net.

I never saw either of my grandmothers bored. If there wasn't an obvious project at hand, they created one. The last photograph of Viola, taken two weeks before she died, shows her crocheting as my father stands by. She was busy until the end. When I'm tired and want to quit, their industriousness makes me push harder.

Viola and Lucy embraced aging as a particular and exhilarating *freedom*. Lucy looked back on her life with gratitude that she had made it through, and done well by her children. Viola would pick apart the past, and remember slights and hurts, but eventually she let go. At the end of their lives, they looked at the whole of it, the gift of it. Worry and anxiety was replaced with a quiet peace. Lucy and Viola had known romance and experienced true love. They accepted their portion and didn't hunger beyond what they had been given. The wise woman knows when enough is enough.

The best years in a woman's life are after forty.

Most of Viola and Lucy's personal accomplishments (outside of their families) were achieved after the age of forty. They used all they had learned, and their experience born of hard work, to *grow*. They never fell into the trap of believing that the breadth and experience of life narrows as it goes on. Lucy raised three college graduates, an astonishing achievement for an immigrant without connections or education. Her son Orlando was a star athlete who had a four-year basketball scholarship to Notre Dame. Her daughters became librarians. The shoe store did fine, and now, alone, she continued working as a seamstress. Her life after forty brought her beloved brother to visit from Italy, and when she could not, her children and grandchildren went home to Schilpario.

Viola's years after forty proved to be the most profitable in the mill. She raised the family and traveled, visiting all the places she dreamed of as a girl. Her marriage settled into the comfort of the long haul. She was surrounded by an extended family of in-laws and she became even closer to her own sisters. It's wonderful to be young, and there are gifts in it, but Viola showed me that experience is the heart of wisdom.

As life goes on, it's experience that sets
the agenda.

You know what to avoid, and what to save, who to share your life with, and who to wish well as you move forward without them. Experience is a gift, as it gives you perspective, it is the great time saver, because it helps you focus on what's important.

If you met Viola, you wouldn't think for a moment that she was sentimental. You might have found her charming, as my friends did through the years, but there was no mistaking the strength underneath. She loved a good fight, and was often engaged in one. This goes back to her days on the farm, where one rule applied to man and to beast: only the strong survive.

Viola's photo album that chronicles her life from the age of sixteen to twenty-seven is filled with pictures of friends, road trips, costumes of the day, and even a shot of the pants factory where she worked. In her youth, as she was beginning to figure out who she was, you could see a longing in her to break free of her responsibilities, find true love, and see the world. When I reconcile the dreams of her youth, and the realities of her life, I imagine that it's in that gap where she became a fighter. She had to fight for everything she got, so her standards were high. She expected my best, and nothing less. She could be critical, and her words would sting. But as her life went on, she softened; her experience had made her more loving, and surely more wise. I asked Viola on her eighty-fifth birthday, which birthday she dreaded the most. 'Stupid question,' she said. 'I only know it's downhill after eighty-five.'

Let go.

Any conversation about beauty these days is centered around what we can *change* about ourselves, instead of embracing what we have been given. Plumped lips can be bought, furrowed brows can be paralyzed smooth, and the entirety of a face can be lifted. We can literally go from sixty back to thirty in a few hours, in the hands of a good surgeon, on the table at the Hospital for Cosmetic Surgery.

But should we?

The aging face might in fact, surprise us – in a good way. We may eventually see those that came before us in our expressions. Our faces will become works of art that our grandchildren will treasure. If we have let go of slights, disappointments, and hurts, that hard-earned and well-deserved serenity will show up on our faces. And what we may love, most of all, about growing older is the purging of the anxiety that comes from trying to please others through the window of our appearance.

None of this is easy, because as women, we *are* beauty. We bring mystery to the world, we're emotional, complex, and full of dreams, and that doesn't change with the passing of another birthday – or eighty of them. Women like my grandmothers remained vibrant in body and mind, and for the most part, it was a choice. Even when her body failed her, Lucy's mind remained clear and her thinking was sharp. She continued to focus on what was working, and live through that, instead of mourning the changes that had come.

Engrave the souls of your children,
not your body.

It would seem that our bodies, in their natural state, are not fascinating enough. The parts must be assigned meaning. If you don't find the curve of your ankle particularly enthralling, you can tattoo it with your choice of Chinese symbols, which will be permanently engraved on your body by a man with a gold tooth who wears goggles as he operates an electric needle that spurts India ink into your flesh. Now your ankle is *saying* something, in addition to holding you up as you walk.

Whatever is natural, it seems, has become mundane. The last thing you want is a boring elbow, a plain forearm, or a hip without instructions. Freckles, moles, and scars are passé; bring on the Sanskrit, emblazoned across your torso like a menu from a fast food joint in downtown Bangladesh. These days, we have a need to make whatever we were born with our version of *better*, and in so doing, leave our permanent wisdom

111

carved on our bodies and not engraved on the souls of our children.

The Italian Nose

I came of age in the throes of 'better living through cosmetic surgery,' and liked the fact that I had options, whether or not I would ever use them. Viola knew of the popularity of cosmetic surgery, but she hoped I would stick with the inheritance in the middle of my face: my nose.

'Never get a nose job,' she said.

'Why?'

'You'll need your nose later. It will hold everything up.' And then she said, 'You'll see.'

She was one hundred percent correct. The nose is the tent pole of the face, and for me, its meaning goes beyond its purpose. When I see my reflection, I see *them,* in my profile and nose: Lucy's strong bridge and Viola's end tip are part of my legacy, and I wouldn't change it now, even if I were offered free surgery. I see everyone that came before me: Venetians on the farm and in the silk mills. I see generations of Bergamasques high in the Italian Alps as they hitched the carriage to the horse in the stable, and filled their baskets with fresh eggs as white as the clouds that passed overhead on a field of Tiepolo blue. I see them all, my people, in their imperfection and their might, right here in the mirror. What is beautiful to me, is not so much what I am, but what brought me here.

If doctors can help you, let them.

Viola's surgical diet regarding noses did not extend to her knees. She had a double knee replacement at New York's Hospital for Special Surgery. The great Dr Thomas Sculco performed the surgery when Viola was eighty-five, and twelve weeks later, when her knees had healed and she stood straight, with marginal post-operative pain, she admitted, 'I should have done this twenty years ago.'

I thought of Viola before she had her knees done. Despite the arthritis and the way they locked in certain positions, she continued to work on the tractor, stand for hours rolling dough and baking pies, prune trees, and shoot her rifle at close and distant range. What if she *had* gotten those knees done sooner? With good knees in her sixties, she might have very well joined the Flying Wallendas in their high-wire act, or danced as the prima ballerina or even become a marathon runner. All I know is she could do anything with bad knees, and with new knees even *more*.

The Flapper

Viola was religious about staying slim. She was a young woman in the 1920s, when the beauty ideal meant freedom. Corsets were gone, hemlines went up, and thin, boyish figures were in, with bobbed haircuts that emancipated women from brushing, ratting, and setting their formerly long hair.

Evidently, young ladies had to be unencumbered to dance on tables and drink gin out of shoes.

In the Roaring 20s Viola was enamored of drop waist chemises and high-waisted, wide-legged pants hiked up with belts, worn with navy-blue-and-white-striped fisherman sweaters inspired by the designs of Coco Chanel. For the first time, women wore pants on a regular basis – the concept of sportswear was born. To emphasize their care-free short haircuts, they wore wide silk headbands or tied enormous bows in their cropped hair. Girls reveled in the freedom of the new wave of fashion, and in the independence that came from their factory paychecks.

A woman's beauty template is determined by the times she lives in when she comes of age. The vision of our younger selves never leaves us. Just as Viola was influenced by the flapper era and the budding It girls of the times, Mae Murray and Theda Bara, my template was defined by the 1980s. I was influenced by Rene Russo in *Harper's Bazaar,* wide strips of black kohl eyeliner smudged under her eyes to emphasize the deep wells of grief that come from being beautiful. Isabella Rossellini made classic features new again. I was grateful brunettes were back – from the Latina on the cover of the Cars album to Esme Marshall, who seemed sporty and gutsy.

I fell in love with trends during my youth, just as Viola had during hers. I continue to trust the power of the shoulder pad, and to this day, I still look at myself in the mirror and wonder if I should stuff the foam triangles into my jackets. So it is no wonder that Viola carried a bit of the Charleston girl in her all of her life, the free spirit who remained slim enough to slip out of a man's arms and through the rungs of a chair and under the table and out the door like a vapor, escaping the vices of the speakeasy.

Viola carried a disdain for excess weight all her life, and would comment to a friend or a grand-child if she thought they had put on a few pounds. This did not make Viola popular, but she was known to be direct and blunt, which was consistent with her managerial style.

Viola was never happier for me than when I was on a diet and hungry. (If this runs counter to her commitment to cook and bake, gather and feed, all I can tell you is that I live with that conun-drum.) Viola was more proud of me when I lost ten pounds than if I had won the Nobel Prize. To Viola *la bella figura* was in fact, *la* slim *figura*, which in turn was *la* best *figura*.

Dr Bonicelli

I never saw Lucy agonize about her figure. Lucy looked at food as nourishment. Her meals were also fresh and homemade. She said you should eat the size of your fist at every meal. You could eat whatever you want, but eat it in small portions. I noticed that there was a balance of fruit, vegetables, and protein in her diet, but here, as in her creations, her discipline appeared effortless. In the afternoon, her snack was a handful of almonds. In the summertime, she kept the pristine white sink in her workroom filled with cold water and bright red radishes, scrubbed clean for snacks.

Each day at noon, weather permitting, she sat for fifteen minutes in direct sunlight, on a break from her work in the shop. Now doctors advise us to do the same, to shore up our levels of vitamin D.

Lucy was so wise about the ways of the human body, she was known in her circle of friends as Dr Bonicelli. Lucy's friends would call her and describe their ailments; Lucy would jot down a few notes and go to her physician's manual, a large, leather-bound blue book that she had brought over from Italy. She would look up the symptoms, and then call back the friend and give them her amateur diagnosis. Of course, she advised the friend to see her doctor. But medicine, health, and natural healing were of great interest to Lucy all of her life.

I keep a box of Bonomi chamomile tea on my shelf because she made me drink it when I had a stomach-ache. I give the same tea to my daughter, and it has the same soothing, calming effect on her as it had on me. I also take Lucy's version of cod-liver oil – omega-3s – and an orange every day. Vitamin C is a great healer, and Lucy recommended it.

116

Do your own chores.

Lucy stayed slim because she did all the manual labor around her home and business herself. No one has ever done an expended calorie graph for the amount of calories burned when operating a wringer washing machine, but I'm sure it's more than a hike on a treadmill. She shoveled the deep Minnesota snow, washed the showroom windows, and cleaned her building top to bottom. She only set foot in a gym to watch her son play basketball.

Walk everywhere.

Lucy never owned a car. She walked everywhere, to the store, the post office, to church, and three miles round-trip out to the cemetery and back to visit my grandfather's grave. There are still folks who remember her long stride and quick gait. Walking was her favorite mode of transportation, and her only one, and she had the long, slim legs to prove it.

When Lucy was felled by a stroke, I visited her during her therapy sessions. She rode a bike and operated pulley weights to build up her strength. Even after her stroke, her embrace was as strong as it was when I was a girl. Lucy was determined in all things, and I remember her example late in life. She could have just given up, but she didn't. She used all her energy to build up her body and get well. I know she didn't feel like taking the therapy, but she did it, and she did it well. There are many mornings when I don't want to put on my sneakers and go for a run, but I think of her and do it.

Waste not.

Viola was in her early fifties when I was born. She was strong, bright, and shiny in middle age, working hard at the factory and determined to save as much money as she could for her future. I remember Viola constantly on the go when I was small. She was firing on all cylinders, at home and at work, and expected the same of those around her. One morning, on the way to the factory, she hit a pheasant with her car. She pulled over, wrapped the pheasant in newspaper, and went on to the factory. That night, she served him for dinner.

The farm mentality never left Viola when it came to her garden and providing food at her table. She grew peppers, tomatoes, onions, cucumbers, and lettuce (and arugula, and collected wild dandelion greens in the spring). She grew grapes on an arbor, from which she would make jams. She made apple cider and table wine. She scoured the woods for raspberries, and went on strawberry-picking expeditions to the local farms. We climbed pear trees, shook peach trees, and gathered apples on the ground to make pies, or boil them down and freeze them in bags to use come winter in cobblers.

Besides her freezer in the kitchen, she had a double-sided freezer in the basement, and in the later years, a freezer chest in the garage. She could literally whip up a meal from fresh vegetables, fruits, and meats she had frozen.

My favorite vegetable was wild dandelion, which we plucked from her fields every spring. She made a fresh salad with the bitter leaves, which were sharp but delicious. By the time spring would roll around and the dandelions were in, I would crave the dark green leaves. My favorite lunch Viola made was called Venetian eggs. She'd line an iron skillet with gravy (her homemade tomato pasta sauce), crack two eggs in the sauce, let them poach, and when they were ready, she would ladle the eggs and sauce over the fresh dandelion, tossed with olive oil, vinegar, and salt. With a piece of crusty Italian bread, it's the most delicious lunch you've ever eaten.

Eat fresh and in season.

Viola's kitchen, her cooking and baking, were determined by the seasons and the cycles of the garden. She planned her meals and baking around what was available and ripe. She said that it was good for your constitution to eat whatever was in season. Fresh root vegetables and chestnuts, roasted or steamed in the fall, canned goods from the garden in winter, dandelion and herbs in the spring, and fresh fruits and vegetables all summer long were the staples of her scrumptious menus. The same went for meat: venison, sausages, and bacon in the winter, roasts from the spring slaughter, and fish from the Jersey shore in the summers (as well as anything she might have run over, like Mr Pheasant). She served fruit fresh and in season: figs and bowls of berries with a side of homemade whipped cream. Viola baked pound cakes in the winter, fruit pies made with rhubarb, sour cherries, and green apples in the spring and summer, and cookies year-round. Viola followed the same cooking calendar as her Venetian mother, cooking fresh with ingredients that were in season. These habits, dictated by the yield of the garden, go way back in our family tree, which, if Viola could have chosen, would have been filled with pears, which she would soak in liquor and serve over fresh ice cream.

No Time to Die

Before Viola died in April of 1997 (from breast cancer that had metastasized to the bone, her doctor told me), she told me a story of something that happened right after my father was born in 1933. She developed, to her despair, welts on her back. They were firm to the touch. The local doctor in Roseto did not know what to make of these welts, so he sent Viola to a doctor who had a practice 'up on Blue Mountain,' part of the Poconos.

The doctor up on the mountain examined my

grandmother and assured her that he had a treatment that would cure these welts. He didn't tell her what the welts were from, only that he could help her. He showed her a glass wand that, when heated, turned blue, almost infrared. The doctor would use this light on her back, and he promised that this light would cure the growths.

Now, I was mystified as she told me this, so I blurted, 'Were they tumors?' And she said she thought so. I asked her why she didn't go into New York City and see a proper doctor, and she said, 'I had faith in this man. And the one thing you need to know about doctors, is that you cannot expect them to cure you unless you believe in them.' So for nearly a year, one day a month, she went up to Blue Mountain to have the doctor give her these mysterious treatments. After one year, the welts were gone and never returned.

Later, when she was diagnosed, I asked her if she thought those welts in 1933 were cancer. She smiled and said, 'If they were, I beat it.'

On Her Own Terms

When Viola was diagnosed with breast cancer in 1996, she opted for radiation and not a lumpectomy and chemotherapy. She drove herself to her radiation treatments. She was very quiet about the diagnosis, and didn't discuss the radiation in detail. This was the only time in her life when I observed her in a state of total serenity. She was practically

121

demure in the face of what would become her eventual demise.

I didn't want her to die. I couldn't imagine losing her.

On the morning of her last radiation treatment for her breast cancer, I met her at the hospital with my aunt. At the end of the session, the doctor and the nurses came out of the room and had a little ceremony for my grandmother. The nurse pinned a small pink ribbon on her collar, congratulating Viola on her final treatment. I remember that she beamed at this small ceremony, so proud. It was if she had been given a diploma, after graduating from college, her highest dream. I'll never forget the look on her face: sheer triumph.

Initially, I begged her to have a mastectomy, and she said, 'I'm eighty-eight years old, and I'm going to die someday, and when I die, I want to go out like I came in. With all my parts.' This was enormously frustrating to me, but eventually I accepted it. No amount of cajoling and begging, even teasing and joking, would change her mind.

I had never seen her so humbled, and so at peace, as she was when she found out she had cancer. I also knew that she wasn't going to change her mind and wake up, like Rocky, and decide to change the course of her life and *fight* with every tool in the doctor's arsenal.

She didn't want anyone to find alternative treatments or call in favors. Viola had done that years earlier when she took her husband to the Mayo

Clinic, and now, twenty-nine years later, she wasn't going to go down that road again. Viola was going to deal with her illness *her* way.

Whether it was her faith, or the confidence that comes from wisdom in the face of the inevitable, she didn't fight what was happening inside her body. Viola was almost relieved to know *how* her life was going to end, and knowing now, for certain, how it would end, she could prepare.

It was then, in her acknowledgement that she was dying, and in her anticipation of the salvation she believed was guaranteed, that Viola became her most beautiful.

CHAPTER 7

SEX AND MARRIAGE

The shoe shop at 5 West Lake Street was a hub during the day, my grandfather repairing shoes, and Lucy sewing for hire. The kids were at school, and vendors would stop in for coffee and chat, and to sell my grandparents supplies. It was a very social work life, made interesting by the characters who frequented the shop.

At night, after supper, the children went to bed, and the Progressive Shoe Shop turned into a social club for my grandfather and his friends. The men played cards, laughed, told jokes, and had a ball. They got loud and raucous, and occasionally the parties went until dawn.

One night, Lucy came down to do some finishing work in her workroom while the card party was happening in the shop. She overheard one of the men saying something off-color about a woman who lived in Chisholm. The men were having a good laugh when Lucy appeared in the doorway. She said plainly to the men, 'I will have none of that talk. You are to respect women and their reputations in this building.' And then she left. I can imagine my sheepish grandfather and his buddies, caught in the act.

Lucy did not engage in gossip, nor did she judge anyone's behavior. She had her standards, but she never imposed them on anyone outside of her family. When it came to her children, she raised them with boundaries to build character, and led them by example.

Lucy was widowed so young that there was certainly an expanse of years to have another romantic relationship. She never did, and she explained why she wouldn't. Lucy felt that all she had in the world besides her ability to work hard and care for her children was her reputation. She knew, living in a small town, that everything she did would become fodder for conversation and affect her children. She never wanted to be the subject of any conversation she wouldn't have wanted her children to hear.

You are your good reputation.

When my grandfather died, Lucy took in alterations from the local department store – men's suits and coats – to earn additional income. The store wanted to send the customers over for fittings. Lucy asked the store to do the measurements there, chalk-mark and pin the garments, and deliver the work to her, and she would return it to them on a timely basis, complete. She did not want to have men in the shop because she felt that it could be construed that she was entertaining men at her place of business. The store happily complied with her wishes because she was the best seamstress around.

Lucy told me, 'You only have one reputation. When your good reputation is gone, it's *gone.*'

Some wisdom Lucy shared with me about romantic love:

- There must be a powerful draw to one another in the beginning.
- It isn't how long you know someone, but how well you can read them, that will guide you going forward.
- Similarities in background and an understanding of where someone comes from give you a good foundation as the relationship grows.
- Do not be afraid to be clear about how you see yourself in the relationship. Do not agree to live in a place that doesn't appeal to you, do not take up work that you don't like just to please him, and make sure that your voice is honored, that you are heard.
- From the start, full disclosure, emotional, financial, spiritual, will help you define your goals as a couple, and help you know when it will be the right moment for you to start your own family.

After Carlo died, Lucy kept a drawer in her room with his things – some photographs, notes, and his clothing. After she put the children to bed (her twin girls often slept side by side with her after my grandfather died), she would open the drawer and cry. Her grief was so all consuming, she worried that she might not make it through. She told me she survived it because she had no choice.

Each night, after supper, she and the children walked to the cemetery to visit his grave. The social custom of *la passeggiata*, carried with her from her hometown in Italy, was a walk after dinner to visit friends and have conversations. Lucy's version had an entirely different meaning in Chisholm.

After about a year, she cleaned out the drawer and began to visit the cemetery on Sundays, instead of walking there every evening. She said that one day, she realized that her grief would never leave her, so she decided to walk with it instead of letting it take over her life. The loss of a happy marriage is one that never leaves you. I can only imagine the glorious reunion my grandparents had when she died. Lucy had waited so long for it.

Lucy would remain a romantic all of her life, but she was never restless for new experiences. For Lucy, there was no such thing as sex without true love, and no romance at all without her husband. The power of one love was enough to fill her heart for all of her life.

I grew up in a different era, when sexual experience was as expected of an adult woman as her ability to drive a car. Religious constraints had lost their teeth. Women felt as deserving of a satisfying sex life as men, and justifiably so. The changes weren't apparent only in the expectations of a woman's personal conduct, but in the family structure as well. As I write this book, the U.S. government just released a report that 41 percent of the babies born in our country in 2008 were born to single mothers. The old order has been replaced by something altogether new.

It's interesting to note, that for all the advances we have made, we still struggle with romantic relationships. American women have been enlightened in every regard, or at least the opportunity for education exists, and yet we still have a difficult time with personal choice, sussing out good apples from the bad, and figuring out how to make love stay after a few months, or a few decades. Maybe indecision and uncertainty are part of the human condition, but we also need to look deeper into our own expectations, and our own definition of what we believe we deserve.

I learned from Lucy that abiding attachment and commitment sustain you. Sex is a gift, not a right. When you find true love, you only have two things to offer: the gift of yourself, and of your time. And the truth is, that's all he has to give you too. If you find yourself dissatisfied, constantly angry, agitated, frustrated, and emotionally spent, if he does not bring out the best in you, no matter how much you love someone, no matter how many lovely moments offset the low points, if you are exhausted, you are not being fed. And if you are not being fed, you will not *grow*.

Self-respect is the most important respect of all.

Look out for yourself. A man who cares about your feelings, roots for your limitless future, and plans to guard your dreams as his own is a person that will make a good life partner. You should not accept less. For Lucy, this meant marriage, in all its breadth and scope. Marriage should make us better, stronger and more focused in all aspects of our lives.

So, with Lucy's moral template before me – and believe me, it often seemed more like an ideal than a version of reality – I began to shape my own opinions on the matter. I read a lot; I figured that if I could find instructions on how to build a canoe in a book, surely there was some writer out there who could help me navigate the tricky waters of dating, relationships, and perhaps marriage. I didn't want my values to be a piano on my back, but rather a bunch of bright balloons that I could clutch for liftoff.

After all, the gift of sex is one of God's very best ideas.

I found the book *Why Love Is Not Enough*, written by the wise and astute Dr Sol Gordon. In the book, when a young woman asks him, 'How will I know when it's true love?' he answers, 'True love energizes you, all the other kinds exhaust you.'

With that revelation in mind, soon I could tell a crush from the real deal, or lust from actual connection. I learned that what intrigued me didn't necessarily sustain me. I learned that attraction was a canapé, and you can't live on those.

It takes time to observe someone who might be worthy of you, and when you've gathered the facts, it's not fair to *you* to pretend that they aren't true. If the man, his world, and his beliefs depleted me, or the life he had built before meeting me left me wizened, I learned to go in the other direction. Sometimes it was easy, and other times it wasn't. I learned from my grandmothers that I had better honor that inner voice. If I didn't, I had only myself to blame.

Soon, it became apparent that to find *one* man in the world in my lifetime whom I could honestly say energized me and made me believe anything was possible wasn't going to be a search yielding a lot, a few, or even *two* possibilities. The world could not possibly be that generous in my regard. The truth was and is, I would find only *one* man who energized me. And I married him.

Where Are Your Beaus?

Viola didn't understand my generation's approach to romantic relationships. We had platonic friendships with the opposite sex, didn't dress up, and in general, it seemed we didn't make a fuss over 'boys.' We called them, asked them out, paid for dates.

Viola wondered, 'What are they thinking?' She felt young women my age were killing romance. 'It was so nice when I was a girl,' she said wistfully.

When Viola was eighteen, there was a social order to dating. Various Venetian families in the area would come and visit on Sundays, ostensibly for coffee and cake, with the side pursuit of offering up their sons as potential suitors for Viola. In the telling, I imagined the farm fields turned into parking lots, with hundreds of young men vying for her attention, like a long line at the OTB that snakes around the block on double-down race days.

Viola made it sound that way.

However, Viola was indifferent about most of the potential matches. She juggled their interest in her nonchalantly, remaining cool and aloof as they turned cartwheels and lined up their roadsters to get her attention. One ardent suitor had pushy parents who wanted their son to marry Viola because they had roots in the same village in Italy. The Perins' eightyacre farm added to the luster of a match with Viola. The young man became vehement about marrying my grandmother.

This fellow became so obsessed that one Sunday afternoon, when she told him for certain that she was never going to marry him, he announced that he was going to hang himself from the tree at the end of the lane.

All hell broke loose. Viola begged him not to do anything dire as her parents and his calmed the young man down. Eventually they did, but it was a source of pride to my grandmother, years later, that a fellow thought he couldn't live without her.

The young man went on to marry happily and have eight children, so evidently he figured it out.

While talk of the relations between men and women with Lucy was centered around romance, the same conversation with Viola was clinical. I had graduated from college and moved to New York City in the early 1980s, so my youth had been defined by the frightening epidemic of herpes (as chronicled on the cover of *Newsweek*) and the tragic discovery of the HIV virus and AIDS. Throw the veil of my Roman Catholic upbringing on top of health risks, and I had every excuse to fear romantic relationships.

As a young playwright who was also part of a comedy troupe, I was losing my friends and coworkers to AIDS as Viola was losing hers to sickness and old age. Our mutual grief bound us together. I was her insight into a modern epidemic that she did not understand.

At first.

Viola would come into New York City when I was working on the cabaret circuit. An enthusiastic audience member, she embraced show people. It was astonishing to watch her mix and mingle with the Village crowd, totally at ease in the cabaret world which included transgender and gay performers, as well as straight kids with Broadway chorus aspirations. She was completely at home with folks who made their living on the stage. I couldn't believe it. Nor could I stop her when she confronted a man who openly criticized my play after a staged reading at the Pennsylvania Stage Company.

Viola said, 'There's a person behind this play. My granddaughter. Right over there.' She pointed at me, I shivered in my Madonna fishnets.

The man shrugged.

'I don't know how you sleep at night.' She shouted as the man got into his car. Then she turned to me.

'The nerve.'

'Gram, you can't take on every person that hates my play. Did you understand it?'

'It was in plain English, wasn't it?'

'Yes it was. But did you like it?'

Viola fumbled for the car keys. 'You're not going to write about our family, are you?'

'Of course not,' I lied. And it's a good lie I've kept ever since.

Viola came to all my plays and cabaret shows. She enjoyed the backstage stories of romances and breakups. She was content for everyone to be free, and find happiness – happy for everyone but me. Viola wanted me to toe the line. Her advice to me in those days sounded a lot like the dialogue from the old movies I watched in revival marathons at the Thalia, the very same ones she enjoyed as a girl when they first premiered.

Nobody ends up in the gutter being picky.

When she wasn't sounding like Norma Shearer in a 1930s melodrama, Viola tried other tactics, including fear. She hounded me:

- Does he make your life better?
- How does he treat his mother?
- Can't you find a nice Italian boy?
- Earn the veil your wear on your wedding day.
- See that white runner? It means the bride is a virgin. (Really, Gram? How did the runner people know the bride was a virgin? Or for that matter – the groom?)
- Once you do his laundry, you're married. You might as well have the benefits if you're going to do the chores.

'I didn't know *anything* when I got married,' Viola told me, directly referring to the sexual relations of mankind.

'How could that be possible? You saw reproduction and birth on the farm.'

'I didn't think *people* did those things,' she said.

The truth is, if Lucy liked the operatic version of True Love, Viola liked the Hollywood version: shiny cars, big promises, fancy clothes, seven-course dinners, flutes of fine champagne, dancing to an orchestra and pitching woo under a paper moon. People in the movies looked divine, probably smelled like peppermint, and were rich, rich, rich. If only life was like the movies.

A woman should have her dream.

'I hope you find a man like my husband.' Viola said to me.

When Viola spoke of her husband, it was with a sense of awe. She couldn't quite believe that Michael Anthony Trigiani had fallen in love with her, even though she had loads of self-confidence and the 1920s version of guts: *moxie*. My grandfather was a catch, and he shared her passion for the good life in the modern age. He admired her ambition, but was also the voice of reason. Often, when I talk to folks who knew my grandparents, they tell me that Viola had the drive, and that my grandfather softened her edges.

My grandfather wasn't a big talker, and he didn't compliment or gush, as some of her prior suitors had done, so she didn't know where she stood with him. Years before she died, I found a small book that she had written in – it contained markings of her piecework in the mill, and a written account of the night her mother died. But there were also some entries about my grandfather. On one page, my strong, independent, fearless grandmother wrote, 'Does he love me? What will the answer be?'

Viola offered up all her best attributes to my grandfather: her ambition, good looks, and charm. She also had a dream for his bright future, and saw a way that she could help him achieve it. She sensed that, married to her, he would excel. And he did, becoming a local politician and serving on the board of directors of the local bank. Viola, it turned out, was not only a blouse maker; she was in the aspiration business. In the best marriages, both parties are in the aspiration business, and when you climb, you climb together, and higher.

Choose wisely.

Both of my grandmothers spoke highly of their husbands, and through their eyes, I thought the world of them too.

They taught me what to look for in a man: from Viola, I learned to look for gentleness, and from Lucy, devotion.

Think of Saint Francis de Sales, who said, 'Nothing is as strong as gentleness, and nothing is so gentle as real strength.'

Carlo called Lucy (Lucia) 'Cia' (chee-uh). Every morning of their married life, he brought a cup of hot black coffee to her in bed. Now, he wasn't the best coffee maker in the world, but Lucy never let on that the brew was lacking. Instead, she told me the story for what it was: a man truly loves you when he does the little things, consistently and with love. Your life should be better for entering a partnership with the person you love. She was not talking about money, but the sense of security that comes from being treated well and with respect.

My grandmothers warned me about making the

wrong choice in a mate, because they knew, as carefully as you might choose, you might just end up with a man who disappoints you.

Speak with kindness.

It starts in the way we *talk* to one another. In my home, I follow Lucy's lead when it comes to arguments. There is no name-calling allowed. No shouting at one another. We have disagreements, but we try and talk things through. As the congratulatory telegram on Viola's wedding day read: *It isn't enough to wear a wedding band; the gold has to be polished every single day.* I was married with Viola's ring to remind me to stay the course. As for Lucy, and her lost ring, it bothered me that it was never found so I sent her a gold band with three love knots bought with my first paycheck as an office temp. She wore it every day, and my mom returned it to me upon her death.

There are no men on the bus to Atlantic City.

While I knew my grandfather Michael, although not nearly long enough, most of my memories of Viola were after she was a widow.

Even in her later years, Viola never believed that she'd lost her mojo with men. When she was pulled over for a speeding ticket when she was around seventy, I was in the car. A handsome young state trooper came to the window, and she proceeded to try and flirt her way out of the ticket.

When he went back to his squad car to check her license, I said, 'Are you kidding?' And she looked at me through her glasses and said, 'What?' And I said, 'Gram, he's maybe thirty. It's not working.' She stiffened in the car seat. 'It is *so* working.'

I leaned back in the passenger seat and cringed. When the cop returned with her license, he handed it to her through the window and said, 'You can go.' She tucked that license into her wallet smugly. Her back straightened, she craned her neck up to check her lipstick in the rearview mirror. I couldn't take this delusion for another second. I felt like I was on a grocery run for chips and vodka with Gloria Swanson in *Sunset Boulevard*. 'He let you off because you're a grandmother, not because you're hot.'

Viola looked straight ahead and said, 'That's what *you* think.'

Later on in her life, she told me that the old magic was no longer necessary. When Viola took day trips on the bus to Atlantic City with her friends, it was an all-girl production. They had a ball, telling stories and laughing about the old days.

'Gram, how great you have your girlfriends. Who needs a man anyhow?'

'You *have* to get married,' she said.

'Why?'

'Because it doesn't last. We've all outlived our husbands. Some of us have been widows longer than we were wives. Go ahead and get married.

138

Have fun.

Get dressed up.

Go places.

Because someday you'll see. It's over. There are no men on the bus to Atlantic City.'

In-laws

In those days, unless you were very familiar with someone, you called them Mrs. I remember Viola and Lucy used Mrs when addressing one another, sending cards, or writing letters.

Mrs Trigiani and Mrs Bonicelli met only once, in the fall of 1956, when Viola's eldest, Anthony, married Lucy's youngest, Ida (a twin, born one minute after her sister), in South Bend, Indiana, on the campus of the University of Notre Dame, on a Monday, October 29.

Lucy was working on the hem of my mother's wedding gown in a hotel room in the Morris Inn. Viola, fresh off the plane in hat and gloves, swept into the room. Lucy told me that they greeted one another, and that Viola wanted to look at the gown. Lucy declined, telling Viola, You'll see it at the ceremony. Lucy was pleasant about this, but firm. She also told me that Viola was very eager to help with all aspects of the wedding, including any sewing, to which Lucy said, 'Mrs Trigiani, everything is taken care of.'

Viola admitted that she wanted to insert herself into the planning of the wedding. Her eldest son was sacrosanct, and she wanted a blowout that was equal to the adoration she had for him. When I spoke to her about the wedding, she said it was lovely . . . and small. Her husband, however, thought it was the best wedding he had ever attended. He thought it was reverent and appropriate.

Gram preferred more of a high-end version of the Italian sandwich wedding or bash – cookie platters on the table, dolls on the roofs of cars, and three hundred-plus in the church. Hats. Gloves. Tulle. Morning coats. Plumes. A band. Mayhem. This was not my mother's desire, so Viola took a step back, which was not easy for her to do.

Lucy's family was humble and hardworking, no flash, all substance. Viola liked substance *and* flash. Her lofty aspirations were never hidden in deed, conversation, or wardrobe. She believed in climbing higher and never looking down. Her material dreams were a mink coat and a Cadillac, and her spiritual dream was eternal life.

However, here on earth Viola admired wealth. If you were rich, it probably meant that you had done something right. Viola was a proud American capitalist. Lucy, while proud to be an American, maintained the Italian work ethic: it was enough to live and provide for your family.

Viola told me that she didn't know my mother when my father sent a letter telling his parents that he planned to marry her. (Dad filled in the details – that Mom was a librarian in the architecture department, that her brother had been a basketball star there in the 1940s, and so on.) This litany of attributes were not enough to recommend my mother as a good wife for my father, Viola needed more information.

So Viola swung into action to find out everything she could about my mother's family. Viola was a big believer in checking your mate's background prior to marriage. This meant meeting the family, including all the cousins, making inquiries, all the while quietly forming an opinion based upon the facts you gathered.

You were to analyze everything about a potential mate: character, education, height, weight, health history, and prison records (hopefully none!). You were to do as much research on 'his people' as possible. After all, marriage was forever, a lifetime lock, so you'd better know who and what you were getting into. I heard her say more than once to a person she had just met, 'Where are your people from?' She knew every village, farm, and barn in her family history, and she expected you to know the same about yours. So in her search to find out about the then mysterious Bonicelli family, she went directly to her local priest.

In person.

The priest in Roseto, Pennsylvania, sent a letter to the priest at Saint Joseph's in Chisholm, Minnesota, inquiring about the family, and specifically about the character of my mother. The letter that came back to the rectory in Roseto was succinct and yet carried some detail. Viola told me that the priest in Chisholm said the Bonicellis were of sterling character, and that Mr Trigiani would be lucky to marry Miss Bonicelli.

Viola was satisfied with the letter (which was sent unbeknownst to my mother, and probably my father), and as the years rolled by, Viola's guarded opinion of the Spada/Bonicelli family changed. It was not lost on me that, years before, Viola's own father had gone to the local priest for the same detective work, with an entirely different result. Priests, it ends up, are often in the intercession business – and not just between the Heavenly Father and the penitent, but also and evidently, between potential mother-in-laws and the women that their sons wish to marry.

Viola and Lucy's differences were obvious in Ektachrome in the costumes they chose to wear on that wedding day. Viola wore an off-the-shoulder, cinch-waisted, full-skirted dress in a shade of blue known then as 'cerulean.' Her dramatic statement hat was wide-brimmed, with a fringe of dyed-to-match ostrich plumes, matching gloves, high heels, and clutch. Lucy, in contrast, wore a neutral champagne colored understated dress with a thin belt that she had made for herself in *peau de soie*, a hefty satin with a dull finish. She accessorized the dress with a small black velvet hat, gloves, and black pumps.

The peacock met the dove.

CHAPTER 8

THE PLACES YOU'LL GO

One of the most frequent questions posed to me as a novelist involves budding artists. Parents want to know what to 'do' with their artistic child. Are there classes? Lessons? Is there something they can do at home to help them find their way?

The most important thing a parent can do when raising an artist is to take them out into the world and show them things. Travel.

Our family stories have it all: risk, adventure, romance, and intrigue. The places my grandmothers came from were described in stories they told. Eventually I would visit the settings of these stories, and they came alive before me. Small-town life seemed exciting. It felt personal and specific. Even a local visit to a friend's house became more than coffee and cake as some piece of news was shared, sending my imagination off in new directions. The villages in Italy were loaded with secrets. There was ancient history, epic romance, and centuries-old vendettas.

My grandmothers took the time to introduce me to people and show me things. Often I was surprised, and sometimes amazed, but never ever bored by the goings-on of adults in real life.

Their worlds seemed populated by colorful characters: In Chisholm, slim Zeke Salvini, robust Mrs Jacobson, and Tootsie Ungaro, in hip Bermuda shorts and cat's-eye sunglasses. In Delabole, Viola had an old family friend named Minna, with a thick Italian accent and a life story worthy of a novel; and as fascinating, her sister Helen (Elia), a hairdresser, a total knockout who married for the first and only time in her forties, and was a second mother to her nieces and nephews when she did not have children of her own.

Family was presented to me as a landscape loaded with characters whose lives had surprising twists and turns, and who grew and changed as the stories of their lives played out. With my imagination populated by these fascinating characters and the things that happened to them, all it took was some education and discipline to find my craft. I mimicked their work ethic, imagining myself in a factory, layering words like tasks until the work was done. I took away more than life lessons from their stories; I made a career out of it.

The Places They'd Go

Lucy, once she arrived in the United States, never returned to Italy. She had a severe form of motion sickness, and nearly died on the ship on the way over. Once she was in Hoboken, she only took

144

one more trip of any length, and that was by train from New Jersey to Minnesota after her wedding to Carlo in 1920. She confined the rest of her travel to her children's weddings, which required days tacked on either end to recover.

When I visited Lucy, her world did not seem small to me, even though she did not leave Chisholm. She never seemed confined; in fact, she walked so quickly everywhere, covering so much ground, that it seemed there wasn't anything she couldn't do or anyplace she couldn't go. Information and news flowed freely into 5 West Lake Street. There was a stack of letters to and from her relatives in Italy, to read, reread, and answer. Her family visited her often; her son and his wife and family lived close by; and the door of her shop was open, with customers and friends coming through on a regular basis.

I told Lucy with high hopes that doctors might invent a pill that would cure her, so she could to go home to Italy again. She'd just smile, as if it were a faraway dream. My greatest joy was when I went to Italy and returned to her with details of all I had seen. I could not have given her a greater gift.

A World of Wonder

Viola had big dreams and loved to travel: cars, buses, trains, ships, and airplanes, it didn't matter, she just enjoyed being on the move. My grandfather did not. He traveled the eastern seaboard of the United States, and always by car. As hungry as Viola was to see the world, Michael loved the quiet of the country and his home. I don't think this was ever a problem between them, and in retrospect, my grandfather took delight in her ambition to visit the places she dreamed of. He encouraged her to go.

When my father was a boy, she woke him at 4:00 a.m. and said, 'I have a surprise.' She and my grandfather loaded my dad and a picnic basket into the car. By dawn, they were on the outskirts of Philadelphia.

They parked their car behind a sea of trucks and took my father's hand. They wove through the vehicles and climbed a small hill to join a throng of people who had come to watch the Ringling Bros. and Barnum & Bailey Circus come to town. My father never forgot the visual of the elephants as they lifted the giant poles to put up the tent. Viola, while she was a strict parent, instilled a sense of wonder in my father. When my father was dying, he recounted that day as one of the best of his life.

Make a big splash.

It also turned out that, wherever she'd go, Viola would make a big splash. Literally. In October 1957 the TWA airplane that carried Viola from Los Angeles, and then to Honolulu, Hawaii, had to make an emergency landing on foam on the runway in Honolulu, akin to the emergency landing made by Captain Chesley Sullenberger in the Hudson River in January 2009. No one was hurt. It was a miracle, the headlines swore.

When Viola told the story of this flight, she remembered everything – the passengers, the stewardesses, the skid into the foam, and the inflatable sliding board where she removed her stilettos before sliding down so as not to puncture the plastic.

My grandfather saw her on the evening news that night, and then, in the days that followed on the front pages of newspapers, sent to him from around the country. It turns out that my grandmother led the rosary on the flight, and she told me that even the non-Catholics chimed in, for extra flight insurance of the heavenly kind.

When she was interviewed by a reporter from the *Los Angeles Times*, she was almost giddy with delight at the success of the emergency landing. Viola didn't panic in the face of death; she prayed.

I am required to fly a lot as part of my job, and when I sit down and snap on the seat belt, I look around and wonder if these are the people that I will be with when I die. But then I think of Viola, and make the sign of the cross and leave my stilettos in the luggage – just in case.

Europe after World War II

Viola went to Italy in 1950, visiting her father's village, Godega di Sant'Urbano, for the first time.

147

With her young daughter in tow, they went to Paris and Rome, and flew back through Dublin.

She returned to Italy in 1970 and visited Lucy's hometown, Schilpario. Viola's gesture meant a great deal to me because it showed respect for my mother's family, and also that on some level, she understood that if Lucy could not go home, it would mean something to Lucy's family to hear firsthand how she was.

Viola had not yet entered her mauve years, the days of winding down, when she relaxed into life, laughed more than she cried, and rested more than she worked. Viola still had the old drive and the wanderlust to travel. To extend herself in this way was very special. Viola seemed comfortable with Lucy's people.

She went to Carlo Bonicelli's birthplace in Vilminore. Our cousins made her dinner, and showed her the sights. She was thrilled to meet Pope John XXIII's brother Zaverio, and took a picture with him. It was as if she'd gotten a photo with Clark Gable at the height of his fame; evidently every American tourist that went to Bergamo after 1965 got a photograph with Zaverio Roncalli.

Just go.

Viola's trips were fascinating to me. She stayed hungry for adventure all of her life, and that inspires me to look for it too, and encourage the same in my daughter. Viola traveled a great deal after my grandfather died, and she never made a fuss about it. She'd invite a friend or her sister-in-law along – she never complained if she had to go alone, she just went. Viola missed out on a formal education, so it was her responsibility to fill in the gaps and see the world that, had she stayed in school, she might have read about in books. A trip or two never satisfied her curiosity; she always wanted to see *more*.

Tiny Bubbles and a Big Kiss

It seemed Viola would drop anything at home to travel, and she also spent a lot of time planning her trips. Through the years, she was game for getaways to the Bahamas with friends. She returned to Hawaii in the 1970s with a tour, with her sister-in-law Mary Farino as her roommate. This time the plane landed safely, the only compromise to her safety (and virtue) came in the arms of Don Ho.

Viola innocently took her place in the queue when Don Ho called all the grandmothers to the stage and into the spotlight during one of his legendary stage shows. One by one, as the machine belched hundreds of champagne bubbles all over the stage, he took each grandmother separately into his arms with a dip, and in a spotlight kissed her. Viola told me, 'Eh. He *really* kissed me.'

Reeling from the kiss, Viola staggered back to

her table. When she looked up, she saw that her sister-in-law Mary, behind her on the line, had received her 'passionate' kiss too, but instead of returning to the table went back to the end of the line for seconds. Whenever I hear 'Tiny Bubbles,' I think about Viola's mini make-out session with the Aloha King, and my great Aunt Mary's do-over.

The Flowered Suitcase

If you love to travel, it's wise to learn how to pack. I still don't have the technique down, but somehow, regardless of the length of a trip, Viola could pack everything she needed into one small canvas suitcase.

Typically there was one nightgown, six count of underwear, three brassieres, one full slip, one pair of stockings, three pairs of footie socks, one pair of bedroom slippers, one set of pumps, one skirt and blouse for church, one pair of slacks, and one additional top. That's *it*. When I marveled at her ability to edit her clothing choices for trips, she said, 'Never pack more than you can carry.'

She carried her toiletries in her purse: toothbrush, toothpaste, face cream, and lipstick. Her 'traveling ensemble' included slacks, a blouse, and flats. She wore a classic trench coat, and in the pockets were a set of rosary beads and two neatly folded, brightly colored silk scarves, which she alternated.

By the time Viola reached her seventy-fifth

birthday, she had developed *sprezzatura*. Lucy had it all along, but life taught Viola nonchalance, and ease was a choice. She began to dress to please herself, and in so doing she developed a style in her later years. Her wardrobe now reflected her simple approach to living.

Viola looked chic and appropriate for every occasion. In the later years, she'd wear her work clothes under a trench coat to mass during the week, and then tuck a colorful scarf around her neck. She'd throw on simple button earrings and wear a rosy lipstick. While I liked her new muted palette of gray, with a shot of color around her face, I missed the drama. The dramatic hats of her youth were gone by her golden years, and I was sad about that.

When I moved to New York City and was barely making ends meet, I did a lot of shopping on the street (still do). A pair of clip-on earrings caught my eye as they shimmered on a blanket on East Fifth Street, and I bought them for her for a dollar. They were round circles of gold filigree with small inset white pearls – good paste costume jewelry. When I held them, I liked the fresh style of the setting and the heft of the fake gold. I gave them to Viola, and she loved them, mostly because I had scored them for only a dollar. She was examining them closely, as they were well made. She said, 'Look at the stamp on these.' So I looked closely; on the clip of the earring, it said 'Schiaparelli.' Viola wore good costume earrings designed by Coco Chanel's Italian rival. She loved that.

Viola Attends Lucy's Funeral in Minnesota

Viola made one last trip to Minnesota in November 1992 to attend Lucy's funeral. It was already bitter cold on the Iron Range. Viola did not make the trip alone; her youngest son accompanied her.

The wake was lovely, with friends stopping by, mostly children of Lucy's lifelong friends. By the time Lucy died, she had lost her beloved son, so my mother and aunt planned the beautiful service at Saint Joseph's Church.

Viola, now eighty-five, herself gave me so much comfort through the funeral, and in the days and weeks afterward. Viola had never known her own grandmothers, and she savored every story her own mother told her about them. Viola had a deep longing her whole life for the lost love she would never know from her grandmothers, and in some ways, when it was her turn to be a grandmother, she struggled with it.

Looking back, I imagine that it had a lot to do with her relative youth (she was fifty when her first grandchild was born), the responsibilities of the factory, and my grandfather's declining health. She took delight in her grandchildren, but there could be a distance, which sometimes felt like disapproval on her part. Viola made enormous celebratory meals, and remembered every birthday and holiday. She made certain that she gave you, as a granddaughter, your first charm bracelet, birthstone ring, and wristwatch. She did everything right, but she wasn't yet comfortable with the easy affection that comes from the distance of an extra generation between grandmother and grandchild. It was obvious that she didn't have a role model in this regard, and she would have to figure it out. But it was to come, and it did, in full circle at Lucy's funeral.

The Little Black Coat

Viola wore a black wool A-line coat with a round collar, covered buttons, and matching piping to Lucy's funeral. She stood with us as we processed into the church. Somehow, Viola's solid presence at Lucy's funeral gave me a sense of hope, even though I knew I had now lost one grandmother, and that someday I would lose Viola too.

Lucy's funeral was moving for Viola; even though they had held one another at a respectful distance, there was an underlying camaraderie. Their Italian roots were buried deep in northern Italy, though Lucy's were high in the snowcapped Italian Alps in a remote but cozy village, while Viola's were in the expansive farm fields of the Veneto, with the Dolomites in the far distance, like hills of salt. They both possessed the take-charge attitude of the firstborn, and both worked all their lives as diligent businesswomen, who never officially

153

retired. They both had an uncanny ability to lead large families, to end arguments, and to encourage good behavior.

Lucy and Viola interpreted the American dream in their own separate ways, but at the funeral, Viola realized they had more in common than she knew. They were small-town girls who knew how to take risks, who loved and lost and believed in a glorious afterlife.

Viola was impressed with Chisholm, how wide and clean the streets were, and how simple and yet substantial Lucy's building was. She liked Longyear Lake and the library. She thought the food at the luncheon held at Valentini's was hearty and tasty. Viola came away with a clear sense of the environment my mother grew up in, filling in the blanks from the letter that the priest had written so many years earlier. Viola liked what she saw.

There were lessons all around that day, if I chose to learn them.

The greatest lesson came from Viola, and is one that will hold me in good stead until I am old. There is nothing we can say to comfort the grieving, but there is definitely something we can *do*.

We can *show up*.

When you stand with someone who is suffering, they will never forget it. And neither will you. So of all the places you'll go, never miss a funeral. These are no longer ceremonies about letting go

154

of the dying, but holding on to tradition, history, and memories. Those who grieve might not even be able to ask, and you might not think they need you, but they do.

I could have gotten through Lucy's funeral without Viola, but I wouldn't have wanted to. Viola's faith sustained me that day, and in her example of traveling to pay her respects to Mrs Bonicelli, I felt a part of *one* family that, when it comes my time, I hope will sustain me too.

CHAPTER 9

CHILDREN

If you love your mother, your child will love you.

Lucy Bonicelli believed that the first five years of a child's life were the most important. The template of care would be set, habits formed, and routine established. The mother learns to *read* her baby and understand his needs as he grows out of infancy into toddlerhood. Before I had a baby, I didn't understand all the conversations about routine. After I had my daughter, I got it. The basics of child rearing begin with getting control of your home and creating structure. This structure is not a version of military efficiency; it's all about giving the baby a world that is secure and a mother she can count on.

In my family, motherhood is revered. I did not go through (many say a healthy period) of challenging my mother or grandmothers' authority. If I disagreed with them, I found a polite way to do it. Italians have statues of the Blessed Lady in our homes and yards for a reason. Motherhood is a sacred club.

A mother shapes family life, and hopefully, she brings what she has learned of her own mother's good habits and common sense to create her own family dynamic. This unbroken chain of gold, from mother to daughter, hands down *priorities* as well as practical advice. Through my grandmothers, I knew *their* mothers, and the kind of values that were inculcated in them.

Bind your child to you.

'Bind your children to you,' Lucy used to say, knowing that when we do so, our children's sense of self is rooted in a deep and abiding security that we are there for them. When a child knows this love and security, you are free to instill values that will build their character.

Routine is not negotiable.

The lessons I learned from Lucy are rooted in common sense. First, and most importantly, a routine must be established. A baby placed on a regular schedule of sleeping, eating, and play will become a secure child who will come to rely upon that routine, and thrive within the boundaries you have set for her. A routine helps the child, but it also helps you *understand* your child. If a child is on a schedule, and her behavior changes, you will quickly realize when something is off, and you'll be able to start pinpointing the problem and deciding on the solution. If your child is listless, when she's usually full of pep, you'll be able to figure out if she's sick, and the severity of it; if she's a robust eater and suddenly isn't interested, or usually goes down easily for a nap, and now won't, a schedule will help you decipher the problem. So much of parenthood is about reading the cues, and responding to them. In the comfort of routine, you will know your child inside and out. Children are happy and confident when they know what the rules are.

Lucy put the children to bed at the same time every night. She believed sleep was critical to the maintenance of good health and emotional well-being. Of course, there are reasonable exceptions to this rule, but the sleep schedule should not change often or much.

Like all new mothers, I felt completely at sea and anxious when I first had my baby. I soon found out that routine, like all the other disciplines in my life, would serve me in my new role as mother. Establishing a daily and evening routine was one thing I could do that I had some sort of control over.

To this day, my daughter is a good sleeper and volunteers to go to bed at night. When I see young children out late at night, or keeping adult hours, and then hear my fellow parents complain that their child is out of control, cross, or cranky, it's no wonder. The child is exhausted. And so are the parents.

Allowing a child to watch television late into the

night is a stimulant. Some will say that the images on the television are harmless, but I completely disagree. You may not find the gunshots on *Law and Order* disturbing, but they will. You are depriving them of more than sleep by keeping them up at night; you are preventing them from developing lifelong good habits around sleep. Let your children develop the delicious habit of falling asleep after bath and book, so they enter the dream state calm and reverent.

Sometimes, after bath and book, Lucia is in bed, and I hear her talking or singing for a few moments. This is her private time before sleep. It's important for her to be alone, to think about her day, and to go off to sleep keeping her own company. One of my jobs as a parent is to guide her so she can be self-sufficient and independent of me someday. Parenting is a temp job. I have just a few years to teach her and enforce healthy habits. A consistent nighttime routine teaches her to develop a capacity to be alone, which I hope will provide her with a well of strength all of her life.

Never strike a child.

When I was growing up, it was absolutely acceptable for adults to hit children to punish them with the ultimate goal of instilling discipline. (It was legal for an adult to paddle a student at my public school.) As a child, I was hit as a disciplinary measure, and I assure you that no good came of it. It did not instill discipline in me, it did not make me a better person, nor did it guide me to right my wrongs, or examine my conscience so I might go forth and behave. It shamed me.

I was a 'high-spirited child,' and in a group, I could be disruptive and silly. My worst transgressions, however, did not warrant a 'beating.' Yes, that's what Viola called them. She never hit me (nor did Lucy), but Viola had a paddle with a photograph decoupaged on the wood of Depression-era children bending over into a barrel. It was as if they had grabbed a few Walton children from my favorite TV show, and asked them to pose.

The threat of the paddle was enough to scare me; Viola did not have to use it. I'd never seen a thing so awful: a glossed-up plank of wood with a hole drilled into the paddle handle for a lace of rawhide knotted on the end, suitable for hanging on the wall.

When I got older, I joked about the paddle, and 'beatings,' but it isn't funny. Under no circumstances should any adult *ever* strike a child (or another adult, or anyone, *ever*, for that matter!). Hitting a child does not encourage better behavior; it creates a cycle of anger in the child, born of the powerlessness that comes from the blows, that when brought into adulthood may go without a name but rises up in other forms,

160

and a deeper sadness that often leads to depression and despair.

The world will be unkind enough to your child (it comes to all of us); she doesn't need those who love her doing the same to her or worse.

Once our daughter was on a routine and began to grow, around the age of three, she began to assert herself. One day we were in her room playing, and she threw a CD down on the floor. I told her to pick it up. She ignored me. I asked her to pick it up. Again she ignored me. Now, I had noticed that my husband had a very clear relationship with my daughter; he was very loving, and also set firm guidelines which she respected. I noticed that she obeyed him when he asked her to do something, like pick up a CD. I did not have the same kind of authority.

So when Lucia ignored me, I said very clearly, 'Sit down.' She looked at me, and got defiant. I said, 'Lucia, sit down.' And angrily, she went to the chair and sat. I took a chair and sat down in front of her, eye to eye. At first she ignored me; then she began to place her toe on the floor like she was going to stand, and I held my ground. She began to cry, and cry, and cry. I watched the clock out of the corner of my eye, and within five minutes, the tears ebbed and she asked if she could pick up the CD, because she was sorry. I tell you this story because somehow, almost without my consent, I had fallen into the trap that I was the good cop, and my husband would assume the role of the bad cop. Unconsciously, I was copying my own upbringing, and yet I knew it wasn't fair, to my husband, to me, or to Lucia.

One of the aspects of motherhood that never ceases to surprise me is how adaptable children are, and how a bad habit can be deconstructed, and reason can rule if we are firm and clear in our goal. That day, I took control, and to this day, my daughter knows the limits I have put in place. Of course, we have our moments, but they are just moments, not a chaotic, angry way of life.

Never ignore a child.

Hitting a child is wrong; ignoring a child is neglect. Smile when they enter a room, put down the BlackBerry and focus. They need our attention; email can wait. It will be there in five years when your children aren't.

Discipline

Discipline is the art of repetition. True mastery of any talent cannot be achieved without it. In every job, regardless of what it is, there are rote steps and drudge work that must be attended to, whether we are painting a house, composing a symphony, or deciphering income tax forms. Discipline is the technique that helps us, step by step, to see the task through and get the job done to the best of our abilities.

Lucy taught me to enjoy the process of creativity. Each step brings particular satisfaction. Visualizing the finished product is the first step. Choosing the components carefully, then executing the design from pattern to final fitting gives the creator a sense of completion. Then, each creation one by one leads to mastery which in turn becomes excellence.

Good manners are not negotiable.

Lucy taught me directly, and through my mother, the importance of good manners. Manners make those around you feel comfortable and feel that their presence is respected.

The first rule of good manners is the *awareness* of the needs of others. To be polite and kind is the hallmark of good breeding. From an early age, I was taught the basics: Hold the door for the person behind you, regardless of age or gender. Be on time. If you can – of course there are times when circumstances make it impossible, and being late once in a while is human. The only time I tack on an additional fifteen minutes on an arrival time is when I'm going to dinner at a friend's house. I know I always need an extra fifteen when I'm a host, so I pay it forward when I'm the guest.

Dining at the table is social, and an opportunity for a child to observe your good habits up close. I never saw my grandmothers eat quickly, gobble food, or swig down a drink. Viola was ladylike, even when she had a beer and cracker after she came in off the tractor. Lucy ate slowly, putting down her fork between bites. The table was properly set in Viola and Lucy's homes for every meal. Neither ate in front of the television set on a regular basis.

Tablecloths for dinner, place mats for breakfast and lunch, a bowl of fruit staggered with nuts as a centerpiece, candles lit, music sailing through in the background – ambience was as important as the right spices in the spaghetti sauce. I learned how to set a table in my grandmothers' homes, and the importance of atmosphere. Eating should not only nourish but soothe and create a construct for conversation. Listening is a star point of beautiful manners, as is inquiring about a guest's family and health. Topics of conversation should *engage*, not *enrage*. Meals are fun, and everyone, down to the baby, should enjoy them. Lucy said arguments at the table made the food poison.

Never burden children with adult problems.

As a widow, Lucy was articulate about what it meant to be alone in making decisions and providing for her family. I told her once that I admired her for all she had accomplished, and she said, 'You do what you have to do.'

Lucy wasn't looking for accolades; she was satisfied that she had made it through, and that her children were good people, raised to adulthood with strong values. She told me her greatest worry was that her children would look back on their young years with deep sadness at the loss of their father. Carlo died on August 24, and on August 28, my mom and her twin celebrated their eighth birthday.

Lucy did not want her children to be afraid, so she was stoic. Part of that stoicism was her nature, and some, she worked at. She would exude strength in the face of all challenges, and at the same time let her children be children. She would never burden them with harsh realities, but at the same time, she did not shield them from the truth of their circumstances. There was no shame in being working people. There was no shame in the struggle. It was not a weakness of character to be the opposite of rich. Wealth was not a goal; rather, providing for the family's necessities – food, clothing (she had that covered) – was the financial victory she worked toward. Survival, with all its pits and woes, was a triumph each and every day. Lucy had an ongoing sense of satisfaction that, step by step, she was making it through. She honored every accomplishment, great and small, and this gave her strength of purpose to move forward.

Do not shame a child.

If one of her daughters wanted her to make a stylish dress, Lucy would take her to the fabric shop and let her choose the material. If the material was too expensive, she would show her an alternative that they could afford, without shaming the girl or making her feel she couldn't have something lovely. Of course, the other vendors in Chisholm knew of Lucy's circumstances, and often would barter supplies in exchange for work Lucy could do for them. Lucy never made a fuss about what she could not give her children. She presented alternatives, and this taught her children to be flexible.

I'm your mother, not your pal.

Lucy's mother had a place of honor in the family, not one of familiarity. Lucy looked up to her own mother, sought her counsel, and followed her lead in all matters at home. Lucy stayed close to Giacomina through letters and phone calls. There was a bond between them that time and distance would not break, but they were not friends; Giacomina definitely had the seniority.

Hopefully, your child will see you surrounded by longtime, loving, and supportive friends. Friendship, and the development of the skills that lead to it, will have been set in motion by example to your children by your wonderful relationship with your adult circle of confidants. You have lived; therefore you have made your friends, choosing them, gathering them on the road of life like daisies.

Friendship is a luscious component of a happy life, and one of the great gifts of being alive. Friends who are your age and around it, who remember the things you do, who share travels and experiences with you, and who carry your insights and secrets through the years, just as you share theirs, are treasures.

Friends who are older, maybe your parents' age or beyond, who provide a mature perspective to your problems and can relate to what you're currently going through, are just as valuable. There is no template for friendship; it is defined by what we like and what we need, what we can give and what we can accept. Enjoy those friends your whole life long, but don't include your children in that circle.

Give your children the gift of choosing their own friends.

As a mother, you need not be one of them. Your child looks to you to lead. Your child looks to you to be wise. Your child looks to you to show her the way. You should be one step ahead of your child, or one step behind her, observing. Your child will have friends to walk with in lock-step, and this should bring you as a parent great satisfaction. You have, in another important way, given your child a good example of one of the fruits of growing up and adulthood – the ability to surround yourself with like-minded people who bring out the best in you.

You gave birth to your child, not to a friend.

Keep your mother-child relationship sacred, and with it the glorious boundaries that shield your privacy and hers. Your child will look up to you, and you will have achieved another milestone in creating a confidence in her that will help her separate from you and achieve independence. If we do our jobs well, our children move on from us and create their own lives, relationships, and families, hopefully, by our example, surrounded by friends who also help them be the best they can be.

Don't sing at the table.

There's an Italian proverb handed down on Viola's side of the family, *Chi e canta a tavola e piu stupido che fuma a letto*, which translated means, 'He who sings at the table is more stupid than the one who smokes in bed.' As a child, this was said to me when I was being silly at meal time. In a sense, it's an aphorism about the importance of boundaries. All Viola had to do was raise an eyebrow, and my behavior went from the Three Stooges to Helen Hayes in *The White Nurse*. When she went for the Italian phrase, you knew you had either performed beyond expectation or were in hot water. When we were at the table, we were there to *eat*, not to perform, or interrupt, or fool around. Therefore, to this day, I don't sing at the table, and I don't encourage my daughter to break into song over antipasto either.

Fill your home with music, flowers, and beauty your child will remember.

Our homes are reflections of what is going on inside us. Lucy taught me to share my home and to have it at the ready for guests.

The most beautiful homes I have ever visited were comfortable, clean, and welcoming. The host was happy to see me, and made me feel that for an hour or two, I could put my feet up and revel in the oasis of calm. It didn't matter about the interior so much. There could be clutter, but good seating to welcome guests. The furniture was comfortable; if something spilled, no big deal and no problem! (I don't imagine anyone feels comfortable putting their feet up in a fancy palace.)

The teapot, handed down, with cracks in the porcelain, did not need to be new because behind it was a family story, told with relish, in hilarious detail. A freshly baked cake for company on a cake stand found at a yard sale is more delicious than any dessert course in a five-star restaurant. When a hostess focuses on her guests and makes them feel at home, you know that when company goes, they have been uplifted by the experience of the host's largesse and calm. Such visits always made me feel that I should try to do the same in my own home.

Do what you can and know that it's just right.

From time to time we feel we cannot entertain company because we can't do it up expensively.

Let go of this notion for the sake of your children. You want your home to be filled with visitors, good friends, laughter, and fun. Choose a meal that isn't pricey and invite your friends over. Let them see you make a nice brunch of French toast, coffee, and fresh-squeezed juice. It doesn't have to be lavish. Have a dessert party. Let your children serve the guests. Generosity is a habit, as are good manners. Teach them how to set up a proper tray, with cups and saucers, napkins, plates, and utensils. A child as young as three can carry cloth napkins from one room to another. Soon you'll be able to give your children a nod when company arrives unexpectedly, and they'll go and make the tray themselves. Think of guests as part of your home life, and soon you will be richer for the experience. Children need to see you in action, making your guests comfortable and showing them that they matter. This habit starts in the home.

Open your home to friends.

These days, folks eat out a lot, so the experience of fine dining is not unknown to us in general. Like you, I can remember dinner parties in the homes of friends far more than any restaurant or party room. There is something about a friend making dinner for others that is special, right from the heart.

Lucy's door was open to company throughout the day. Built into her workshop were two easy

170

chairs that faced her sewing machine. She'd put down her work and enjoy a cup of coffee and a slice of sponge cake with her visitors, who dropped in regularly and unannounced. These visits brought the world outside into Lucy's shop. Everything was discussed there, and yet kept private. If you told Lucy a secret, it went no further. Lucy made every person who came into her shop feel valuable and important. This is the first lesson of parenting that she taught me. Every child is important – every single one. And by extension of that, so is every person you meet.

Support your child's interests and talents.

The basic needs of the child must be met, and just as importantly, the parent must figure out how to nurture a child's individual voice. This enterprise is often trial and error: violins came and went at Lucy's home, and sports across the board were played, until her son winnowed down his athletic prowess to basketball. Once my uncle's amazing athletic talent became apparent, Lucy worked with him on the ideals of sportsmanship and fair play, leaving the development of her son's athletic skill to the coach. To this day, when I meet men who played with my uncle, or saw him play, they comment on his manners, his sportsmanlike conduct, and his leadership under pressure. This was a credit to his mother.

Without a father in the home, Lucy had to

171

navigate how to raise a son by herself. Without close family nearby, she had to lay down the law, but also make her children feel they were not alone. She reached out by making herself a reliable member of the community. She stayed front and center in business, and the good people of Chisholm provided her with an extended network of people who cared about her children and their well-being.

The friends who were Lucy's friends before she was a widow remained close and constant. Her children had strong male figures to look up to, and the very same men kept their father alive with stories of things that he had said, and things that they had done. The Ungaro, Sartori, Bonanti, and Latini families stayed close, and through the years, the children's father was not forgotten but celebrated through these strong men. Lucy's determination to provide security for her children extended to their individual needs.

Self-education is a lifelong commitment.

Lucy went to the library regularly, until she could no longer walk there. Public libraries are the jewel of small-town life, a place to gather and exchange ideas, a place that welcomes you if you're alone and looking to read a light, entertaining story. The Chisholm library housed various newspapers from around the world, knowing the town's immigrant population appreciated reading their news in their native languages. There was an innate respect in American libraries for immigrants, and a sensitivity to their needs, and the families they had left behind. The public library system contributed to the ongoing education of immigrants and welcomed them whole-heartedly to pursue knowledge as part of the American way of life. My grandmother could not fathom Chisholm without a library, and wherever we live, we should not either.

When you can, walk.

Viola would often save her money and walk instead of taking the trolley from Pen Argyl to Bangor. From a young age, she equated physical labor with 'clearing her head.' A long walk was therapeutic; her body was engaged, so her mind was free to sort through the demands of the day ahead, or to reflect upon her work on the way home. It's good for the body and the mind, and to pass the time, Viola often repeated prayers by saying her rosary. This form of meditation soothed her, and was a habit she maintained until she died.

Earn your place in line.

Every summer in Roseto, Pennsylvania, the church sponsors a festival in honor of Our Lady of Mount Carmel. In the last weekend of July, a carnival and celebration culminated in the Procession, a parade of believers saying the rosary in honor of the Blessed Lady who watched over their community and protected them. Viola was a member of the Ladies' Sodality, who were front and center in the parade, walking behind an elaborately embroidered banner with the crest of their organization sewn into the silk. The ladies of the sodality walked two by two, and occasionally mothers or grandmothers in the group would let their daughters and granddaughters walk with them, even though they weren't members of the organization. When I grew old enough to understand, I asked Viola if I could walk with her, and she said, 'No.' I brought up other girls my age who were walking with their grandmothers, and she said, 'You have to earn your place in the procession.'

I was annoyed at the time, and probably hurt, but I grew to understand the wisdom of her position. In every possible way, Viola tried to teach me that every stage of life, and every stage of commitment, has its compensation. I was not a member of the sodality, I had not done the work, so I did not deserve to go to the front of the line. Yes, I would be welcome to walk in the very back of the line with the parishioners and visitors who had no affiliation within the church, knowing that over time, it would be possible to earn my rank by hard work and contribution, if I dedicated myself to the spiritual rigors and works of mercy required to get to the front of the line, but not before. Viola wasn't going to give me that right, I had to earn it. Viola was setting an example, and like all good grandmothers, she knew that was the most valuable thing she could do for her grand-daughter, who was watching her up close and emulating aspects of her behavior.

Let children see you do for others.

I spent a lot of time in hot cars in summertime waiting for Viola while she visited a friend in the hospital and I wasn't yet old enough to go in. I rode shotgun in her station wagon when she'd hand off a bag of oil pretzels to leave inside the screen door of one of her old friends who worked in the mill. I helped her count and tear raffle tickets she was selling to raise money for the school. I'd crawl up the side of an embankment on the side of the road to cut wild and free tiger lilies so she could make a vase of flowers for a friend in the hospital.

Viola was always busy doing things that no one could see, acts of grace and charity. I almost believe she didn't want anyone to know of her generosity, expressed in big and small ways, because it would undercut her tought reputation. Sometimes I see a pie plate on a stoop or a note on a screen door and think of her.

Never complain about your physical ills.

I would visit Lucy after her stroke, when she lived in Leisure Hills Health Center in Hibbing, and the ride back down to the Twin Cities in my rental car was always awful. My last visit with Lucy was more difficult than any that had come before, because she told me that she was at the end of her life. She asked me to promise her that I would not cry, that I would be happy for her sake. I asked her if she was afraid, and she said she wasn't. 'I cannot understand why God gave me such a long life.' And then she lifted her hand that had been paralyzed by the stroke with her good free hand. 'Can you believe it?' she said.

At the end of her life, Lucy died of natural causes. She had a heart issue and was in the hospital, and when she woke up, she was surprised that she was still on earth. Shortly after, she went back to Leisure Hills, and there, she decided to let go. She ate less and less, slept more and more, and eventually she passed away on her own terms, in her own way, quietly and with dignity.

Her friends used words like 'serene' when describing her. The local paper reported her as 'grand.' Lucy had every reason to be angry, petty, and indifferent, because she had in many ways been cheated. The loss of her husband, and then her beloved son, who died seven years before she did (and this was a son who visited her twice a day, every day of her life), and the loss of her physical ability from the stroke, which meant she could not live alone and at home anymore, seemed like tragedies even for a woman who loved her solace. But my grandmother didn't complain – not about the pain, and not about the loss. When I visited her, she wanted me to get out and do things.

She didn't want me to sit around with her – she wanted me to go and see things and come back and tell her about them. When I did, she would light up, relishing in every detail of my day. In a broader sense, this is what it has meant to be a writer. I go out, experience the world through characters and conversation, hopefully fetching the good stuff, the details that surprise and bind us, then bring all of it to the page. Lucy encouraged me to do the same for her.

Perhaps Lucy didn't complain because she didn't want me to look at life as anything but a journey full of possibility and wonder. She wanted me to have the joy she had known, without any of the sadness, knowing that was impossible, but wishing it so nonetheless. From her, I learned the very definition of love: when you truly love someone, you want the best for them, and their happiness is more precious to you than your own. When you love someone, you are on their side and take their part, believing them and fighting for what they need.

For Lucy, the harsh realities were not negotiable, but her reactions to them could be. She was not about to burden me or anyone else with the difficulties of what she was going through. She took her elderly years one day at a time, but it was not easy. That was her road, and she could handle it alone, as she had all the loss in her life. Lucy was not defined by that sadness; having lived it, it belonged to her. She walked with it, made peace with it, and eventually she was even free to let it go. She certainly had no intention of sharing those burdens with me. She wanted more for me, better for me. But what she could never know, even though I tried to tell her, was that I was better for having known and loved her. She lit up when I came into a room, but my heart burst just as full at the sight of her. I hope I see her again.

CHAPTER 10

BELIEF

Just a Dream

Dreams were fascinating to my grand-mothers and to me. We discussed them and analyzed them. Of particular interest were the dreams that included visits from those who had died. In fact, after the proper period of mourning a loved one has elapsed, the first question I ask is, 'Has she visited you?' Or, 'Has he?'

One of Lucy's most poignant losses was that of her mother. Lucy had left Italy at the age of seventeen, with the hope of returning home to Italy in a year or so. She sadly never returned, and she never saw her mother again. But one autumn night, October 3, 1950, asleep in her bed in Chisholm, she had a vivid dream in which her mother appeared to her at the bottom of the stairs of 5 West Lake Street. The dream was so clear that Lucy sprang out of bed and ran down the stairs, thrilled to embrace her mother. When she realized it was just a dream, she went back to bed. The next day, her brother called, informing her that her mother, Giacomina Grassi Spada, had died in Schilpario. The grief that consumed Lucy stayed with her for the rest of her life.

Viola shared a similar experience. One winter night in 1929, Viola was preparing to go to a dance in town with her sister. Her mother had been coughing, but they assumed it was nothing serious. It was bitter cold and snowing outside, but Viola insisted she was going to the dance. She had a new purple drop-waisted dress that she couldn't wait to debut. Viola loved Saturday nights; the band, the beaus, and the respite from her working world in the factory. Viola could be glamorous and gay and full of fun when she was off the clock. She and her sister set out for the trolley to go into town. Viola was twenty-two years old.

Word soon reached Viola and her sister at the dance that their mother had taken a turn for the worse. Viola rushed home, and she and the family gathered with the priest at her mother's bedside. As my great-grandmother got worse, the priest, Father Ducci, prayed on his knees, next to the bed, through the night. A doctor arrived, only to deliver the devastating news that nothing could be done. Giuseppina Covre Perin died before dawn the next morning, at the age of forty-three, mother to six children, the youngest, Lavinia, only five. Viola ripped the purple dress in two and vowed to never wear purple again, as it had brought tragedy upon the family.

My great-grandfather was bereft. On the morning that they returned from the funeral, a local farmer came to the house and pounded on the door. When my great-grandfather opened the door, the ashen-faced neighbor insisted that he had seen my great-grandmother walking in the field along the property line between his farm and theirs that morning. Knowing it was impossible, they still clung to the hope of what the neighbor had seen, and the entire family set out on foot to find her. They tried to imagine that the worst had just been a dream and that they would all soon awaken and she would be with them again.

Viola said the reality of going up into the field and looking for her mother, and not finding her, was devastating. Viola begged God to bring her mother back, but when He didn't, Viola moved on to grieve for the loss of her mother her whole life. She shared the pain of this deep sorrow and regret with Lucy.

A good mother is irreplaceable.

The Infant of Prague

One day, I was with Viola, and she drove past a yard sale. She hit the brakes hard and threw the car into reverse. Her daring behind the wheel of a car was something to experience, I promise you. Something had caught her eye in the yard sale. She backed up in front of it and handed me a five-dollar bill. 'Go and get the Infant of Prague,' she said. I reluctantly got out of the car, went to the lady holding the sale, and asked her how much she wanted for it. The seller wanted five bucks for the statue and the costumes, but if I didn't want the costumes, the statue was three bucks. I went back to Viola and explained the terms, and she told me to buy the entire Infant of Prague kit, clothing included.

When I got back in the car, Viola pulled out on to the road. This wasn't a good statue. It wasn't like the Italian, hand-painted plaster version Viola had in her living room, with artful velvet costumes to be changed on High Holy Days. The orb the Infant held was cheap, and the overall effect was more poolside decor than chapel-ready.

'Gram, this is the worst Infant of Prague I have ever seen.'

'I couldn't leave him there.'

'What do you mean?'

'A sacred relic in a yard sale is *not* right.'

Now I have the Infant to remind me of that day, and now I too cannot part with it. I have placed a Post-it on the base of the statue: Do not put in yard sale.

A Green Mountain

A couple of weeks before Viola died, I stayed with her. Now, this is the strange thing, looking back on this night. She knew the end of her life was coming soon, but I was going to convince her it was not the end. The more I tried to lift her spirits, the more agitated she became. Finally she dozed off, and I soon did too. At one point, she cried out. I woke up and turned on the light. She said, 'I'm in so much pain, I can't even cry.'

So I said, 'Well, let's not try and sleep. I'll go and get you a snack.' I went downstairs, made tea and bread and butter, and brought it to her. Viola was not a touchy-feely person, and I never saw her reach out and stroke someone's arm or pat their hand. She would hug me, but with a coda of quietly pushing me away with her hands after a few seconds. And when it came to kissing, she'd just extend her cheek, and I'd kiss *her*. It's how I imagine affection is shown in the royal family in Great Britain. There was never anything fussy about Viola's affection. It was slightly military.

But I knew she was in agony, and I knew from my Reiki sessions in New York City that rubbing someone's feet can be a tremendous source of pain relief. When I was a kid, the washing of the feet on Holy Thursday was the greatest challenge for me, as I found the entire exercise hilarious, even thought the priest explained that this is what Jesus did. For me, it was just another example of how difficult it was for me to be Christ-like. But tonight, she needed it, so I rubbed my grandmother's feet.

'I had the strangest dream,' Viola said. 'There was a very tall, green mountain, and your grand-father was at the highest peak.'

'Was he young or old?' I asked.

'Young. Like the day we married. And he said, "Come with me, Viola." He was smoking a pipe.'

(I knew the pipe well, and the Blackjack tobacco he used to pound into it. Once in my twenties I followed a man smoking a pipe for three blocks up Sixth Avenue when he was smoking the same brand, just so I might remember this detail of my grandfather.)

Viola continued, 'And I began to head for the base of the mountain to climb it, and there in a rocking chair was an old woman. When I got closer to her, I saw that she was one of the machine operators at the mill. She pointed for me to follow my grandfather up the mountain. I said to her, "But what about you?" And she said, "I stay here."'

Immediately, in my denial and zeal to be peppy, I chirped, 'Well, they're helping you get well.'

Viola looked at me and said, 'I'm not going to get better.'

I remembered visits when I was a teenager, and how I used to check and make sure she was breathing at night, afraid she would die. And one night she caught me and told me that she used to do the exact same thing with her grandfather, Jacinto, who emigrated when he was eighty-eight years old to live with his son and his family. Jacinto lived to be a hundred and one years old. One night he woke up, and she told him in Italian, 'I just wanted to see if you were okay.' And my great-great-grandfather said to Viola, 'When you are old, someone will take care of you, because you took care of me.'

I was trying to take care of her now. But I didn't

184

feel good about it, I felt helpless. The tea was cold, and the bread and butter was too much for her to eat. She tried, but then pushed it aside.

And then I asked her the biggest and most looming of all questions when a person is dying: 'Are you afraid?'

I pictured all those mornings she went to Mass, and all the rosaries she said, and how her lips would move silently saying the Hail Mary as she cooked. And how she said 'Jesu, Jesu,' when she heard bad news. And how she'd ask anyone for money when raising it for the church, and how she'd make you buy a ticket to the annual Cadillac Dinner. And how when you needed to sell raffle tickets for a fund-raiser, she'd take a stack and sell every single one. And how she'd bake a pie and leave it for someone sick, and how she went to every single wake and funeral, whether she knew the person well or not, whether she actually liked them or not. Her reasoning was: everybody should have a standing-room-only funeral. And how no matter when you dropped in, she could make you a feast from a bare cupboard – bread and salami, an egg in marinara tossed through greens, peppers thrown into a skillet with onions and a piece of sausage on the side, a glass of wine, crisp ginger cookies in a tin with hot coffee – there was always something for you, something for the unexpected guest. I thought of how she'd cut the grass at my grandfather's grave, hauling an actual push mower in the back of the station wagon, me praying that we wouldn't hit a curb and explode in a butane fire from the tin gallon of gas at my feet, the nozzle stuffed with an old rag. And how she'd put flowers on her husband's grave every week until she died, and trim the weeds, and wash the headstone. And how suddenly it was *her* turn. I didn't know what I would do without her. I was so sad, I actually thought, I won't be able to do *anything* ever again once she is gone. I'd trade my future to have her here forever with me.

I wanted her to tell me that she wasn't one bit afraid, that this dying business was as natural as getting your hair done or sewing a hem. And I already knew that while it may have been natural, it was also lonely. I couldn't do the thing for her that she'd done for me. I could not make her feel secure when she needed it the most. Viola knew it, and I knew it too. She was on her own.

She said, 'You know, Adri, you get to this point, and you can't pray anymore.'

'Sure you can.' I tried to be upbeat. Again. I reminded her of the First Fridays, the novenas, the rosaries. How about the old God Help Me? Three little words. How hard is that? 'Come on, Gram. *Pray.*'

'I can't. I've tried. The one thing I thought I could do, I can't do anymore.'

'Well, Gram, I guess that means I have to pray for you.'

She looked at me, and her expression was so funny that I laughed. 'I know, me of all people.'

'Yeah, you.'

And we laughed. We could always laugh.

Tumult

There is such tumult around religion. God is supposed to be in the blessing business, and indeed He is, but then, when bad things happen, when horror gives way to tragedy and then to loss, what are we to make of it? Isn't religion supposed to help us?

Arguments about religion come at us from all sides – many that make sense, some that merely incense, and others that make a believer feel helpless and alone, which of course is the exact opposite of living in the limitless possibility of the human spirit. Wars are started in the name of religion, but sometimes other things start wars too: money, land, energy sources, and the explosion of long-festering jealousies. Religion is supposed to be all-inclusive, but pretty soon a list is revealed of folks who aren't welcome inside those bright red doors. What we do to one another as human beings is often terrible. Our capacity to love, however, is greater than any differences we have, or the labels we are slapped with, or the lines we are asked to form – or at least, that's what I tell my daughter.

I grew up in a southern coal-mining town, buried deep in the glorious Blue Ridge Mountains, where less than 1 percent of the population was Roman Catholic. A poor missionary order of priests and

187

nuns called the Glenmary, whose mission was to serve in the poorest places in our country (Appalachia qualified), is still there, fighting the good fight and ministering to the people of the mountains. Their mission of serving the poor and seeking social justice in all things (employment, politics, fair play) and their devotion to honoring the land and the creatures that inhabit those majestic mountains are honorable and decent, and pretty basic. Not too many folks would argue with them.

I understand what it means to be a minority, and to defend a set of spiritual ideals that are just beginning to form. For as far back as we go, my family has been Roman Catholic; it is as much about being Italian as it is about religion. You can find out most any fact you need about my lineage by checking church records. But even then, with all this history behind me, I wanted to decide what I would be for myself. I wasn't sure who I was in the eyes of religion, but I always knew who I was in the eyes of God. I didn't like to be in the position of defending my church. This was something I was born into, not something I had chosen for myself. I felt that I should be allowed to seek God however I wished. I thought I should atone for the sins I committed, not the ones others said I had committed. I was often torn, and in spiritual exile. But those Glenmarys – they got me. I saw how they did it. It was plain, it was simple, and it was grassroots. It was person-to-person. And I realized, and now have seen many years later, they don't even need the building. They don't even need the costumes. All they need is a circle of folks who want to be still, and there it is, in the gathering of a few in prayer – the celebration of faith.

I am not a theologian or an expert in any matters of religion. I have been exposed to many, and found a deep beauty in the history and traditions that are at the center of organized religion. I remember moments at the wedding of my Jewish friends, who at the reception sang a beautiful song they had learned from a cantor as kids. I've shared Seder supper during Passover in Norton, Virginia, and then with the Luck/Schneider family in New York. I made a good Muslim friend in Annika in South Africa during Ramadan, and learned, by watching her, the beauty of sacrifice through fasting. The great sects of the Protestant Church – I've taken delight in their celebrations, covered dish suppers, and devotion to alleviating human suffering and being present for the poor. A Baptist funeral is a send-off to behold; it almost makes you believe that grief is a good thing.

And I've seen the other side too – when God, and your notion of Him or Her, is used to manipulate earthly want. Well, it's enough to make you throw your hands up and forget religion altogether. Organized religion is complex, and there is much good to recommend it – a sense of community, of connection, of purpose. The grassroots work done in the name of God in the Appalachians by the Glenmarys is practical and also transcendent. However, structured, organized religions are run by human beings, so our capacity for good can be well matched by lesser traits, and sometimes even evil.

The development of faith and a spiritual life that sustains us is not about religion; it's something far more personal; it's about cultivating the ability to be *still*. We must nurture our souls with the same diligence with which we care for our bodies, and in the same fashion that we have built our intellect through the development and study of ideas and the celebration of our particular gifts and skills. We cannot simply walk in this world subject to the whims of fate and materialism, of greed and want, of fame or recognition, or of grief and despair. We have to be strong inside. When we have fortified our souls, when we have taken it upon ourselves to be responsible and to honor the dictates of our own conscience, strength comes.

I watched Viola work through the despair that came when her three-year-old granddaughter, Michalynn, died of leukemia. I watched Lucy stoic and supportive when her grandson Paul was diagnosed with severe autism. They led our families with grace. They moved us forward.

We know how to love one another, to take in love, to return it. We know when it's right because everybody wins; everybody is better for the exchange. The depths of self-love come from the connection we make to our souls. If that connection is made, if we become aware of the force of the unseen, we cannot be swayed to go against the voice within us. We will hear it, and we will do the right thing.

Always.

The finest people I have ever known never went to church, or went and don't go now. The finest people I have ever known might go to synagogue once a year, or on occasion stop in church to light a candle; still others make sure they go every week. There is no one path to learning to be still. You use the tools you have, and if that includes gathering in community, then that's for you. Some people go to the gym, and others put on a pair of sneakers and run as far as they can go. Both build the body, and so it goes with the soul, the path to faith is personal.

I cannot separate out the dutiful Catholic from the imperfect one, or the agnostic from the atheist, or the diehard Presbyterian from the cultural Jew. No one belief system, or lack of one, has the ticket to the concept of heaven with a guarantee that Saint Peter is there to punch your card and send you in. But there is a difference in people who have the ability to be still, and go inward and keep their own counsel. They have *peace*.

As Sister Bernie Kenney (a nun who is also a nurse and operated the Saint Mary's Health Wagon for years in the Appalachians, delivering medicine to people who had none, and a modern-day saint according to Father John Rausch) said to me, 'There are no labels on the other side.' Hopefully, we won't act like there are on *this* side either. But somehow, it's an ongoing struggle – when we are adults, the invisible dividing line remains, akin to what we experienced in the high school gym at school assembly: different beliefs often represent strains of humanity, and not the whole. You have the popular, the artsy, the geeky, the jocks, and subsets of all; but in religion, it's *worse*. Sometimes religious leaders believe they are above us, and that's when exploitation and evil take root to destroy the very beliefs that we hope will sustain us in our quest for inner peace.

How do I acquire this inner peace? Just as the sustenance of anything that matters to you takes care and diligence, focus and attention, it takes daily commitment. Each day we must carve out time to go inward, to embrace the silence and listen to the voice within. Some spiritual people find this voice through the physical – they break through to their souls by using their bodies to focus on a particular thought, or a goal. Others immerse themselves in the service of others, and in so doing, find the still voice in the strength they need to serve. We all come to it our own way, and if we are wise, we pay attention to everything that comes our way that opens our hearts. That's really all it takes.

I learned to pray as a Catholic girl. The mysticism, the prayers, and the rosary in particular matter to me. The greater goal of serving others is never far from my mind, though I come up short often and plenty. But I know how to pray, and I can thank my religion for that. I learned how to be still watching my grandmothers. Sometimes they were so busy caring for their families and doing their work, they had to steal a moment to be still. But they did it; they *insisted*.

I found rosary beads tucked in their pockets, and prayer cards in their wallets, and small books of wisdom, dog-eared and marked up, on their night-stands. They owned the destiny of their souls, knowing that there was very little of the physical world that they could control. Loved ones would die, money would come and go, friends would disappoint, family would hurt, disaster would strike, but nothing that ever happened to them would catch them unaware and render them helpless, because they knew how to pray. They knew how to be still, and tap the state of knowing that deep within you are all the answers you need, and an endless well of strength that will sustain you. This is spirit. And it has nothing to do with the pew you sit in, or don't.

I'm sure they hoped I would be a good Roman Catholic, but more than that, they hoped I would be able to listen to my inner voice and follow my heart. One led to the other for me. Who knew that trusting the voice would give me a job that I love and would sustain my family? Who knew that trusting the voice would help me make the best choice of lifetime partner, with the promise of commitment giving way to romance and hopefully, lots, greater, and even better sex? Who knew that trusting the inner voice would give me one good daughter and a peek through the window to the future in her eyes? This inner peace has also given me the ability to navigate grief, pain, loss, disappointment, and tragedy. I know it's not about me; it's about how I *react*. And when I am experiencing the worst – and believe me, it shows up uninvited – I turn to the voice within. I rest in the notion of that peace, and no matter what, the voice tells me that it will all be all right.

You can find chapter and verse to back up God's big plans for us, and tell us that if we follow a few choice beliefs, those beliefs will lead us home. That might be true, but none of these promises can be realized without the ability to go inward. And truthfully, when it comes to the concept of God, I only know that He made me, and maybe that's all I get. This life.

The gift of this crazy, fabulous hayride is mine, which, if I'm lucky and pay attention, will be shared with family and friends who want the best for me, and I for them. Then as a bonus, the ordinary moments that are also divine: standing in front of a blue ocean, holding your daughter in her pajamas on a winter morning when she's not quite awake, or writing one good sentence in a sea of seven hundred pages of trying, reveal themselves like lone glittering stars on the darkest night sky. The gifts, in fact that keep on giving: the promise that you are not alone in this insanity, that you can love someone and hold on. But you need *strength* to hold on. The ability to be still gives you that particular strength, and the power to appreciate and, for a second, to *hold* the moment. If I get to the other side, and I find out that indeed that was the prize all along, I will spend eternity in bliss.

I could only know these gifts because of the stillness.

At the end of Viola's life, I asked her if she had any regrets. She said, 'I wish I would have had more children.' And I was shocked – after all, she'd had four children, which seemed like a lot. And furthermore, at that point, in the spring of 1997, I had none. Having a child was on my mind, and I suddenly felt bereft that she would never know my children. But I also knew that you can't plan everything, even if you try. So instead of telling her that I was sorry that she would never see my children, instead I asked, 'Gram, why more kids?' And she looked at me and said, 'Because life is good.'

And then she smiled.

AFTERWORD

We worry what to give our children, agonize about what gifts to give them in the hopes of choosing something special that will build a memory for them. We trudge to theme parks, take them to musicals, unveil the wonders of the circus or the thrill of carnivals to give them an *adventure*, where they have to be brave while having fun. We want them to remember the blinking lights, the whirling Ferris wheel, and the glass boxes filled with spools of pink cotton candy. We want to give them moments, so hopefully, when they're old, they'll look back and remember the commitment we made to their childhood, to *show* them things, to fill their imaginations with wonder.

We hope they'll remember the thrill of riding on Mr Toad's Wild Ride, or maybe they'll forget the ride, the circumstance, the day, and simply remember the feeling of security they had while holding our hands on the endless line. Maybe that's the best gift we can give them, the knowledge that we will always be there. Or maybe it's the only gift that matters.

After Viola died, I went to visit her grave. I drove down to her house in early summer, when trees were in bloom, and the house and property were hidden by foliage. As I made the turn up the driveway, I felt she was there. I took a walk around the grounds, remembering the summer days, the chores, and our conversations. I used to address my letters to her: 'Mrs M. A. Trigiani, Head Nun, Little Sisters of the Poor Summer Camp.'

I got back into the rental car and drove through the village, and into Bangor, and up to the stoplight. I was thinking about her when there was a tap on the passenger window. I looked over and saw a man. I rolled down the window, thinking he might need directions.

'Are you Viola Trigiani's granddaughter?' he asked.

'Yes. You know she passed away.'

'I saw it in the paper.' He introduced himself.

'You know, she came to see me before she died,' he said. 'I live in that house right there.' He pointed.

I remember his house because next to it was an impromptu alley, a strip of grass with grooves made from the wheels of parked cars, two parallel dirt tracks with tufts of grass going between them.

The man parked his cars in the alleyway. And they weren't just cars, they were vintage models. There was a beauty, one that I admired since I was a girl. It was a hardtop Ford Fairlane circa 1960 in mint condition. My favorite aspect of the car was the wide turquoise-and-white harlequin shapes on the sides of the car. It looked like Commedia dell'arte pantaloons to me. Whimsical. And whenever we drove by, I'd look for the car, and tell my grandmother I wanted that car. Then we'd spar.

'What would you do with that old car?'

'Put it in your garage.' I'd tell her.

And then we'd argue about the car I didn't own. There wasn't room in the garage, and besides, why should she be stuck with another vehicle to maintain? How would I afford it? Why would I need a car when I lived in New York City? The car was old. You never know about old cars – they might look good on the outside, but be clunkers on the inside. And on and on. It was a routine with us.

The man looked at me as though he knew what I was thinking.

'Were you the one that liked my Fairlane?' he asked me.

'Yes sir, I was.'

'Well, last March your grandmother knocked on my door. Said she wanted to buy the car. I told her I wasn't selling it. She tried to bargain with me, but I stood my ground. Then she went soft and told me that it was for her granddaughter, who admired it. I was moved, but I still wouldn't sell. She left me her number in case I changed my mind.'

I thanked him.

'I think it's nice she wanted to by it for you,' he said.

I couldn't say anything. I was thinking that a car was the highest gift you could receive in the Trigiani family.

On the way to the cemetery, I thought of all the things my grandmother did in the weeks before she died. She gave things away. She dropped a herringbone car coat at her niece Violet Ruggiero's house, because Violet had admired it. She made amends. She called her friends. She invited her grandkids to play cards with her in the hospital. She took visitors. She pretended not to be in pain, and when they'd sneak booze into the hospital, she'd toast them from a plastic cup.

In her final days, Viola made life seem like a party that shouldn't end, whether she stayed or went. I thought about the girl she had been, one who loved dancing, parties, and a life of glamour and fun, but whose path turned serious when her mother died so young.

Her passing made me aware of precious time. I was lucky to have time with my grandmothers. These moments are my treasure, afternoons or mornings or bits of time at a family function when I was lucky enough to steal private moments with them. In my imagination, these moments swirl around one another and clump together; the days and years might somersault over one another, out of order and out of sync, but the message remains clear.

I was loved, and I loved them.

Whenever I wish, I can taste their cooking, hear

their laughter, and know their love, just as they promised.

When I was young, I worried that they would die. The thing I feared most didn't happen, I was lucky to have them both into my thirties. They didn't see my daughter born, but I'm pretty sure they sent her to me.

And greedily, when they died, I wished for more. There are days when I would trade everything I have to be with them again. But I've learned that there is never enough time with someone you love. *Ever*.

I look down at my hands a lot, and remember theirs – Lucy's long, tapered fingers as she sewed, and deftly spun the wheel on the Singer, and Viola's hands, at first artful and strong, and then in constant motion to ward off arthritis. Their hands did not rest; they were busy creating, stirring, crocheting, pruning, or kneading. When I attempt to follow their example and make something with my hands, whether it's a meal or something crafty, I come in a distant second to my grandmothers, but I *try*. I owe them that.

I learned how to be a woman from my grandmothers. They taught me their simple definition of feminism: make your own living. Rely on no one to take care of you. When a man controls the checkbook, he controls you. Be a good partner, an equal, and demand that he be a good partner too. Work for yourself, invent your own business, so you can set productivity, pace, and therefore profit. Pay your bills. Clean up your debts as you go; let the obligation to pay off the debt fuel your ambition. Own your own home. Have a moral code that elevates your thinking, and your behavior will follow. Use common sense. Modesty is the guardian of privacy. Defend your good reputation; you can't get it back once it's gone. Apologize when you're wrong. Fight back when wrong is done to you, or to those you love. Loving one good man is enough. Know that you will see all those you have lost again, and beat back sadness with the knowledge. Take care of your parents, honor their wishes. Have a purpose and beauty will follow, you won't have to work at it. Style is appropriate. Know what you like, cultivate your individual taste, and you won't care what anyone else thinks. Fill a vase with fresh flowers from your own garden. Grow lilacs near a window, and your home will be filled with springtime when they bloom. Good manners are insurance that you will be invited back. Leave your children your values, not *stuff*. Do not be afraid to die, it's natural. Take a chance, and when you fail, take another. There is no limit on risk; aim high and aim true. Be bold. Be direct. Be different. Remember who you come from; you owe them because they *gave* you the ticket to this adventure. Honor the debt.

I try to live these mandates, and I fall short plenty. But I want to show my daughter how to live, not just tell her. Words evaporate in thin air like smoke, but actions galvanize the spirit and reinforce good intentions. I want to leave Lucia the intangibles – the gift of going inward, an example of peace and of connection – knowing that it is these things that will nurture her soul and make her strong.

Women have found a way to survive and thrive that is unique to our sex. For me, and I trust for many of you, your philosophy of life, your approach to living, came from your relationship with the sages in your life, those women who came before you and made you feel you could achieve a great thing or master a small one, and either would be met with encouragement and then approval. Hold their wisdom close and follow their example.

Maybe your sages didn't come from your family. You might have been close to a teacher, or a boss, or a neighbor who taught you how to make something, and in so doing, taught you how to *be* someone. It never, *ever* occurred to me that I wouldn't work, and that if the fates were kind, I wouldn't be gifted a family of my own.

Love your work, enjoy it. Hard work is good for us. Lucy and Viola loved their work; the mastery of their crafts brought them a sense of satisfaction. Work gave them something that they could in turn give to me: *drive*. Ambition fuels purpose, and purpose builds character, and character sustains a strong family. When it appeared that a task was dull, or that the development of a technique in my chosen profession could be repetitive and boring, they upped the stakes and encouraged me to push harder. They knew that a plateau was only a foothold upward to something greater. They turned this slog into an adventure.

I miss them.

I will long for the cool summer mornings when I'd go berry picking with Viola in the woods. The sun was barely up, but it threw just enough light to see. Raspberries grow deep in the brush, and you have to hunt for them. Sometimes we'd look and look, and no luck. I'd tell my grandmother that maybe there weren't any raspberries this particular year – maybe there'd been too much rain, or not enough. 'Have you checked the *Almanac*?' I'd complain. Viola would ignore me and push me deeper into the woods, and farther into the forest, certain we'd come upon them. I wasn't so sure, but I followed her anyway.

Over and over again, we bent back spindly branches thick with leaves, hoping to find them. We'd trudge up a gnarly path and push through more foliage, hoping for a glimpse of red. When you found one cluster, you knew that it would lead to the mother lode. This particular boondoggle seemed like a gold rush with no payoff. I wanted to give up.

There were often thorns and sharp spikes growing in the bushes to turn us back. The slushy mud pits under the green gave me the creeps. I wondered what weird animals lived in the forest – what if one bit me? There was only a dried-up bottle of Mercurochrome and some old gauze in Viola's crap emergency kit from 1932. I wondered if she thought about *that*. But Viola was determined, so I kept looking too, if only to prove to her that this year, there weren't going to be any raspberries.

I offered that she should put up something else – grape jam or apricot jelly. How about peaches? We had a couple of crates of those that her sister had dropped off. I even said, 'Let's just go to the store and buy berries.' With that, she looked at me and glared. I was missing the point.

Just when I thought we'd never find them, she pushed back some dense green vines and there, embroidered into the thicket underneath, were the raspberries. There were hundreds of berries, sweet and plump, ripe and ready to pick, just like Viola promised, just as she had hoped. She let out a whoop! The pirate had found the buried treasure, the long-lost wedding ring suddenly appeared, and when you were penniless in a downpour at 3:00 a.m, you found a bonus twenty-dollar bill hiding in the bottom of your coat pocket to get you home. It might as well have been a million! Yes, Viola had struck oil, tapped the vein, and hit the jackpot. The raspberries had been there all along, and I almost missed them. They were buried deep, and full and perfect, just like rubies. And just as priceless.

FROM ADRIANA'S KITCHEN
RECIPES INSPIRED BY OUR TABLE

My grandmothers were wonderful cooks, bakers, and hostesses. I think of them whenever I am preparing to entertain. Before my guests arrive, I straighten up the house, pay special attention to the powder room (candles, guest towels), arrange fresh flowers, set the table with a mix of lovely china and heirloom glassware, stagger and light votive candles in their crystal holders on tables and mantels, set out cocktail napkins and colorful dishes, and hit the dimmer switch. I make sure there are pillows and throws set around in case anyone gets a chill. Lucy taught me that the comfort of my guests is my first priority.

Lucy and Viola taught me to make a sacred space for guests, and then all you need for a memorable evening is the most delicious food in the world, simply prepared and served with grace. As I wrote this book, I reveled in the handwritten recipes that Viola and Lucy left behind.

On the Spada/Bonicelli side, my mother, Ida, and Auntie Irma have wonderful memories of Lucy's sponge cake, a staple after Sunday mass.

Lucy used to make the gnocchi (a recipe from her mother in the Italian Alps of northern Italy) for her growing children. My uncle Orlando swore that gnocchi was one of the reasons he grew past six feet tall!

On the Perin/Trigiani side, Viola's friends remember the Oysters Rockefeller, the sumptuous cakes, the appetizers, and the 'delish' cocktails (Viola used the word 'delish' as a supreme compliment – it meant 'You must try this!'). I found the Queen Elizabeth cake recipe folded neatly in her files, and I reprint it here as I found it. As you can see, Viola's good work extended to her kitchen, and her trusty cake pans raised money for her beloved church Sodality.

I also have added recipes from a beautiful lady I met on March 6, 2011. Bruce Castellano wrote me a lovely letter about his beloved mother, May, and his aunt Dotty, who lived together on Long Island. The *girls* (as he called them lovingly), age eighty-nine and ninety, wanted to meet me, so I invited them into the city for lunch. Bruce let me know that May's health was failing, so I offered to visit the girls at their home. When I arrived in Greenvale on that Sunday, I was greeted by a high-energy former teacher, Marie (May) Tota Castellano, and Dorothy (Dotty) Tota, a manager for most of her career at Cartier.

Their niece Jeannette Siano Newman and son/nephew Bruce joined us for an unforgettable afternoon. We sat in May and Dotty's blue-and-white kitchen at a large, comfortable table situated under a skylight. The rain poured down as we talked about books, politics, social justice, men, life, and cooking.

They served a glorious feast of Italian sandwiches, biscotti, *scatallate* (see the recipe on page 216) with hot coffee. My sister and friends Elaine and Dee joined us, and soon the party had wings. May gave me her philosophy of life, and I toured her elegant blue bedroom (very Mario Buatta) connected to a sitting room filled with books. I marveled at her collection of novels and biographies, history books, and cookbooks. I was thrilled that we had similar libraries, and simpatico taste in authors. We looked at her mother's handmade wedding gown with delicate beading from 1919 and family photographs through the years.

What a gift that afternoon was to me.

I write books to remember the stories that I never want to forget, the details of faces, the technique of how to make this or that dish, and to hold close those memories that sustain and fulfill me. I write these books for you, and in some small way, I hope these stories encourage you to write down the memories that mean something to you. Lucy died in 1992, Viola in 1997, and there isn't a day that goes by that I don't turn to them in memory, because the truth is, even though they are gone, I still need them as much as I did when they were alive, and as you know, there are days when I need them *more*.

I am asked, why would you spend a Sunday afternoon with May and Dotty, two women you never met? I can't give you a simple answer. I have learned that so much about making art, creating stories and writing novels, is about honoring those instincts that lead you home. Something told me that May and Dotty had something to tell me, and the least I could do was be a grateful guest in their lovely home and share the experience of their table and their life stories.

I don't have my grandmothers to lean on anymore, and it could be surmised that I am looking for them still, in the eyes and experience of women of their time, women like May and Dotty. But it may be even deeper than that. There are no strangers on this journey. The values instilled in me from my grandparents were the same as May and Dotty's parents had for them. Education, family, faith, love, cloaked in respect and justice for all was their way of life. May and Dotty found threads of their past in *Lucia, Lucia; The Queen of the Big Time*, and the Valentine books. They had so much to tell me. When I walked the halls of their home, the walls were filled with art, glorious paintings created by Carmelo Charles Castellano, May's husband. When I left them that afternoon, I was energized. May had Bruce give me a few recipes, and I include them here. I left with tins of *scattalate*, sandwiches for the journey home, and limoncello. I remembered whenever I left Viola and Lucy, they would load me up with tins, things that they had made, food and drink to sustain me. And it was the same with my new friends May and Dotty.

May died on April 3, 2011, just a month after our visit. How happy I am to have met her and Dotty. But now, you can know them, too, as you make their recipes.

DELISH COCKTAILS

All recipes serve two, because Viola believed no one should drink alone. *Cent'Anni!*

Viola's Signature Sweet Manhattan
(Serves 2)

4 ounces whiskey (We like Maker's Mark.)
6 ounces sweet vermouth
3–4 dashes grenadine
Maraschino cherries to garnish

In two tumblers filled with ice, pour the liquor and grenadine. Gently stir. Drop two cherries in the glass and serve.

Viola's Fuzzy Navel Base
(Serves 2 in the shade)

4 navel oranges for squeezing
4 ounces peach schnapps
Fresh mint to garnish

Make your orange juice fresh by using a hand press. Cut the oranges in half and squeeze, drain juice into two glasses filled with ice. Add peach schnapps and stir. Garnish with mint.

The Front Seat
(Viola's redo of the traditional Sidecar)

3 ounces bourbon (We like Kentucky Colonel.)
1½ ounces Cointreau
Juice of one fresh lemon

Shake ingredients gently in cocktail shaker filled with ice cubes, hit a pot hole and shake well. Strain into a chilled glass.

Viola's Highball in Low Weeds
(Perfect after mowing the lawn)

4 ounces whiskey
1 8-ounce can ginger ale
Lime to garnish

Fill highball glass with ice, add whiskey, and top with ginger ale. Garnish with curl of lime (for the weeds).

VIOLA'S APPETIZERS
Serve with the cocktails

Ham and Cheese Ribbons

25 slices yellow American cheese
25 slices *capicola* (spiced ham)
25 slices Muenster cheese
16 green olives with pimento centers (sliced thin)
⅓ cup horseradish, drain well

On a slice of yellow cheese, spread horseradish, then ham, more horseradish, then top with a slice of Muenster cheese.

Trim edges. Cut stack in four squares, then into triangles. Garnish with slice of green olive with pimento, secure with a toothpick.

Refrigerate.

Viola's Spanish Olives

3 cups large green olives
1 cup vinegar
1 cup olive oil
1 green chili pepper, sliced
1 clove garlic, minced
1 teaspoon oregano

Place ingredients in jar, marinate overnight, refrigerate, and serve.

Sables for Girls Who Wear Minks

1 cup flour, sifted
½ cup butter
1 cup Parmesan cheese, grated
1 teaspoon salt
Fresh pepper
Fresh cayenne
2 tablespoons water
1 egg, slightly beaten

Preheat oven to 400 degrees.

Combine flour and butter. Add cheese, salt, pepper, and cayenne, mixing with fork. Sprinkle with water. Roll into ¼-inch thick balls and cut with biscuit cutter.

Place on ungreased sheet and brush with beaten egg.

Bake 12 to 15 minutes until golden and serve hot.

MAIN COURSES

Lucy Bonicelli's Gnocci di Patate

5 pounds baking potatoes
3 teaspoons salt
1 large egg
1 cup flour

Gnocchi is a dish that requires some practice. The success is about creating the right density in the mixture that becomes the small dumplings. Peel the potatoes, boil them in salted water. When they are cooked, put aside and let them cool. Mash them with a spatula, and beat in the egg when the potatoes are room temperature. Slowly add the flour until the potatoes become doughy. Add more or less flour as you see fit. Then roll the dough on a floured cutting board. Roll out ropes of the dough the thickness of a pearl necklace. Cut the dough into 2-inch pieces, corrugate the pieces, creating waves. Boil 8 quarts of saltwater. When it is boiling rapidly, drop in a few of the gnocchi.

Let them cook briefly in the boiling water, scoop them out with a slotted spoon, drain them in a strainer, and place them in a bowl. When all the gnocchi are cooked, serve with sauce. Choose either sauce for your fresh gnocchi:

Lucy's Sage and Butter Sauce

½ stick butter
½ cup cream
Roasted sage sprigs (6 or 7)
Dash of cinnamon
¼ cup Romano or Parmesan cheese

Melt butter, cream, sage, and cinnamon on the stovetop, stirring as it cooks. When foam appears around the edges, ladle over the gnocchi. Sprinkle with Romano or Parmesan cheese.

Lucy's Quick Tomato Sauce

4 fresh garden tomatoes
1 pat butter
¼ cup olive oil
Pinch of salt
¼ cup Parmesan cheese
Fresh basil leaves, shredded

Chop tomatoes, cook on stovetop with butter and olive oil until the tomatoes glisten. Add pinch of salt, sprinkle with Parmesan cheese, and finish with shreds of fresh basil on top.

Marie (May) Rita Tota Castellano's
Pizza Rustica

INGREDIENTS FOR CRUST

1 pound (approximately) flour
3 level teaspoons baking powder
Pinch of salt
3 eggs
3 ounces olive oil
½ cup warm water, or as needed

Make a well of 3 cups flour, baking powder, and salt on a board. In the center, place eggs, olive oil, and some of the water. Mix these ingredients lightly with a fork. Gradually add more flour and water as needed to make a soft, tender dough.
Allow to rest, covered, to be rolled out later.
In the meantime prepare the filling.

FILLING

1½ pounds full cream ricotta
4 eggs
¼ cup or more Italian parsley, chopped
Fresh ground pepper to taste – no salt
¼ cup Parmesan cheese, grated
½ pound prosciutto, sliced then chopped
½ pound sweet dried sausage, sliced then cut in half
½ pound mozzarella, chopped
1 basket cheese, cut up

Preheat oven to 350 degrees.

215

Mix ricotta, eggs, parsley, pepper, and grated cheese in a bowl.

Butter a deep 10-inch round pan (I use a spring-form pan for easy removal). Roll out ⅔ of dough to cover bottom and sides of pan. Place a thin layer of ricotta mixture on bottom. Then layer meats and cheeses (mozzarella and basket). Repeat layering with ricotta mixture and other ingredients. Try to end with a layer of ricotta. Cover with the remaining rolled dough and seal edges. Brush with beaten egg. Cut some vents in top dough.

Bake in oven for 1 hour and 15 minutes. Test center with a thin knife blade. It should come out clean. Remove, place in cake rack to cool and remove side of pan if using a spring-form pan.

May's Cartellate
(aka Scattalate)

4 cups flour
4 eggs
½ cup sugar
¼ cup vegetable oil (Mazola)

Make a well of the flour on the baking board. Mix in the eggs, sugar, and oil with a fork. Mix well, drawing in the flour gradually. Knead well and let dough rest, covered.

Either roll out dough a fourth at a time very thinly or put through pasta machine – passing the dough several times at thinner openings, kneading the dough.

Cut dough into ribbons 2 inches wide with a fluted pastry wheel and cut each into about 4 inches long. Cut a slit in the center and pull one end through it making a bow tie.

Fry briefly to a light color turning each in hot oil at 360 to 370 degrees. Remove to paper towels on a cookie sheet.

These can be served with a sprinkling of powdered sugar or *vino cotto* when close to serving time.

Viola's Oysters Rockefeller

2 dozen oysters (shucked, meat only)

MIXTURE
¾ cup butter
¼ cup onion, chopped
¼ cup celery, chopped
¼ cup parsley, chopped
¼ clove garlic, chopped
½ cup bread crumbs
½ cup spinach, chopped
½ cup watercress, chopped
Pinch of salt
⅛ teaspoon hot pepper seasoning

Preheat oven to 450 degrees.

Place the oysters in 8-inch-by-10-inch glass baking dish. Mix ingredients for the mixture and spoon it on top of the oysters.

Bake in oven for 10 minutes. Serve individually in shell dishes. Garnish with watercress.

DESSERTS

Marie (May) Rita Tota Castellano's Biscotti con Madorle

1 cup almonds, shelled and toasted
1 stick softened, unsalted butter
¾ cup sugar
2 eggs
½ teaspoon vanilla
2¼ cups flour
2 teaspoons baking powder
½ teaspoon salt

Preheat oven to 325 degrees.

Finely grind ½ cup of toasted nuts; separately crush the other half.

Butter and flour a 10-inch-by-15-inch cookie sheet, or use parchment paper.

Cream butter and sugar, beat well. Beat in eggs and vanilla, beat well.

In a bowl, sift flour, baking powder, salt, and ground nuts. Add flour mixture gradually to egg mixture in mixer. Beat well.

Remove from beater and, by hand, mix in crushed nuts with a wooden spoon.

On prepared cookie sheet, form dough into two rolls about 16 inches long and 2 inches wide.

Bake in oven for 30 minutes, until lightly gold. Remove and cool without moving the rolls. Remove from sheet and cut diagonally about ½-inch thick. Spread on same cookie sheet, cut side up. Bake for 10 minutes, turn, and bake till golden. Cool (about 26 to 27 minutes).

Viola's Pot De Créme

1 pound sweet chocolate
3 cups light cream
½ cup sugar
12 egg yolks, slightly beaten
2 teaspoons vanilla

Melt chocolate in cream in a double boiler. Add the sugar and stir. Gently add in the egg yolks, stirring over the heat, until the chocolate mixture thickens. Add the vanilla. Pour into small ceramic cups, refrigerate, and serve with whipped cream.

Use the leftover egg whites for a facial while the pot de crème sets. Beat the egg whites and dab on to clean skin. When the egg whites tighten the skin, rinse with cool water.

Viola's Icebox Cake
(Serves 5)

1 package sweet chocolate, melted
1½ tablespoons water

1 egg yolk, unbeaten
1 tablespoon confectioners' sugar
½ cup whipping cream
1 egg white, stiffly beaten
12 ladyfinger halves

Blend the melted chocolate with water. Add egg yolk and beat until smooth. Mix in the sugar. Whip cream and fold into chocolate. Fold in beaten egg whites. Line an 8-inch-by-4-inch-by-3-inch loaf pan with wax paper. Layer wafers with chocolate mixture. Chill overnight. Unmold.

Queen Elizabeth Cake

1 6.5-ounce package chopped dates
1 teaspoon baking soda
1 cup sugar
½ cup butter
1 beaten egg
1 teaspoon vanilla
1½ cups all-purpose flour, sifted
1 teaspoon baking powder
½ teaspoon salt
½ cup chopped nuts

Preheat oven to 325 degrees.
Pour 1 cup boiling water over chopped dates and baking soda. Let stand while the rest of the ingredients are mixed together.
Add mixture to the dates, mix, and place in 8-inch-by-12-inch or 9-inch-by-9-inch pan. Bake

about 40 minutes. (Check with straw after 30 minutes to see when done.)

ICING

5 tablespoons brown sugar
5 tablespoons cream
2 tablespoons butter
¾ cup coconut
Chopped nuts

Boil first three ingredients for 3 minutes. Add about ¾ cup coconut and some chopped nuts. Spread on cake, and return to oven for about 10 minutes, until coconut is golden brown.

Note: This is reportedly the only cake that Queen Elizabeth herself makes. This is not to be passed on but must only be sold for charitable purposes for 15 cents.

Viola's Fluffy Golden Cake

2½ cups flour, sifted
1½ cups sugar
4 teaspoons double-action baking powder
1 teaspoon salt
½ cup high grade shortening
1 teaspoon lemon extract
½ teaspoon vanilla
1½ cups milk
5 unbeaten egg yolks

Preheat oven to 350 degrees.

Sift together flour, sugar, baking powder, and salt. Add shortening, lemon extract, vanilla, and 1¼ cups of milk. Beat. Add the remaining milk (¼ cup) and egg yolks.

Divide mixtures into two greased and floured 9-inch pans. Bake 30 to 35 minutes.

Viola's Spice Cake

1 cup raisins
¼ pound margarine
1¾ cups flour
1 cup sugar
1 teaspoon baking soda
1 teaspoon cinnamon
1 teaspoon nutmeg
1 teaspoon cloves
1 pinch of salt
1 egg
1 teaspoon baking powder

Preheat oven to 350 degrees.

In a pot over low heat, cook raisins in 2 cups water for 10 minutes. After it comes to boil, add margarine. Let cool.

In a bowl, mix the rest of the ingredients. Add in the raisins, margarine, and water. Bake for 50 to 60 minutes.

Rhubarb Pie

PLAIN PASTRY PIE CRUST
1½ cup all-purpose flour, sifted
½ teaspoon salt
¼ cup shortening
4 to 5 teaspoons water

Sift flour and salt in bowl. Slowly add dollops of shortening into the mixture, forming tiny balls. Add water slowly until the flour shortening mixture is damp. Separate in two equalsize balls on wax paper (for upper and lower crust). Chill for 3 hours.

Roll pastry lightly on floured board until it's ¼ inch in thickness. Roll from the center, so the crust is the same density throughout. Roll each ball into a sheet.

RHUBARB FILLING
3 cups rhubarb
1 cup sugar
2 tablespoons flour
⅛ teaspoons salt
2 eggs

Preheat oven to 350 degrees.

Peel rhubarb and cut in ½-half inch pieces before measuring out 3 cups.

Mix sugar, flour, salt, and beaten eggs in a bowl. Add to the rhubarb and pour into the pie pan.

Grease pie plate, place the large sheet of dough in the pan. Add rhubarb mixture. Place second sheet on top, trim the edges to fit the pie plate. Pinch the dough around the edge of the pie plate, creating a ruffle. Make small slits in the top to allow steam to escape. Bake for 10 minutes. Reduce heat to a moderate oven (325 degrees) and bake 25 to 30 minutes.

Lucy Bonicelli's Sunday Sponge Cake

6 egg yolks
1 cup sugar
1½ tablespoons lemon juice
6 egg whites
1 cup pastry flour
¼ teaspoon salt
1 teaspoon vanilla

Preheat oven to 325 degrees.

Beat egg yolks until thick and lemon colored. Add sugar gradually and continue beating. Add lemon juice and fold in the stiffly beaten egg whites. Fold in the flour and salt, mixed and sifted together. Pour into a tube pan and bake for 50 to 60 minutes.

CONVERSION TABLES

The tables below are only approximate and are meant to be used as a guide only.

Approximate American/ European conversions

	USA	Metric	Imperial
brown sugar	1 cup	170 g	6 oz
butter	1 stick	115 g	4 oz
butter/ margarine/ lard	1 cup	225 g	8 oz
castor and granulated sugar	2 level tablespoons	30 g	1 oz
castor and granulated sugar	1 cup	225 g	8 oz
currants	1 cup	140 g	5 oz
flour	1 cup	140 g	5 oz
golden syrup	1 cup	350 g	12 oz
ground almonds	1 cup	115 g	4 oz
sultanas/ raisins	1 cup	200 g	7 oz

Approximate American/ European conversions

American	European
1 teaspoon	1 teaspoon/ 5 ml
½ fl oz	1 tablespoon/ ½ fl oz/ 15 ml
¼ cup	4 tablespoons/ 2 fl oz/ 50 ml
½ cup plus 2 tablespoons	¼ pint/ 5 fl oz/ 150 ml
1¼ cups	½ pint/ 10 fl oz/ 300 ml
1 pint/ 16 fl oz	1 pint/ 20 fl oz/ 600 ml
2½ pints (5 cups)	1.2 litres/ 2 pints
10 pints	4.5 litres/ 8 pints

Liquid measures

Imperial	ml	fl oz
1 teaspoon	5	
2 tablespoons	30	
4 tablespoons	60	
¼ pint/ 1 gill	150	5
⅓ pint	200	7
½ pint	300	10
¾ pint	425	15
1 pint	600	20
1¾ pints	1000 (1 litre)	35

Oven temperatures

American	Celsius	Fahrenheit	Gas Mark
Cool	130	250	½
Very slow	140	275	1
Slow	150	300	2
Moderate	160	320	3
Moderate	180	350	4
Moderately hot	190	375	5
Fairly hot	200	400	6
Hot	220	425	7
Very hot	230	450	8
Extremely hot	240	475	9

Other useful measurements

Measurement	Metric	Imperial
1 American cup	225ml	8 fl oz
1 egg, size 3	50 ml	2 fl oz
1 egg white	30 ml	1 fl oz
1 rounded tablespoon flour	30 g	1 oz
1 rounded tablespoon cornflour	30 g	1 oz
1 rounded tablespoon castor sugar	30 g	1 oz
2 level teaspoons gelatine	10 g	¼ oz